I0446770

Women In Negotiation

(W.I.N)

*__Women In Negotiation (W.I.N): The Female
Five – Our Negotiating Superpowers__*

Copyright ©2023 by Blu Bonsai Inc.

Editor: Chisom Ezeh

All rights reserved. This book or any portion thereof may not be reproduced or used in any manner whatsoever without the express written permission of the publisher, except for brief and direct quotations in a book review. Information contained within this work of nonfiction is strictly for educational purposes. The ideas, opinions, and philosophies expressed herein are unique to the author. Should you test, apply, or use any of the concepts within this book, you take full responsibility for your own actions.

www.blubonsai.com

The Female Five
Our Negotiating Superpowers

W.I.N examines 5 key Negotiation Bedrock Concepts, the characteristics skilled negotiators exhibit with respect to those concepts, and the distinct advantages women have to win in the negotiation arena.

Women In Negotiation

(W.I.N)

THE FEMALE FIVE - OUR NEGOTIATING SUPERPOWERS

SUSIE MALONEY

Contents

Everything was Different.
Nothing had Changed.

It was 1991, and I was warming up for my dressage test at the PANAM Games, which was also the selection trial for the Olympics the following year.

The field was abuzz. Horses were dancing all around, circling on their haunches, cantering sideways, trotting on the spot. All were preparing for their 5-minute dressage test, which would set their positions for the Cross-Country the following day and peg their placement for the entire competition.

Equestrian sport has long been stamped 'The Sport of Kings.' If you were not already aware, looking onto the field that morning left little doubt as to how fitting that name truly was. The horse's coats were so clean; they were shiny, reflecting the morning sun. Their manes were tightly braided. Their tails were trimmed at the buttock, perfectly groomed, and flowing with the wind. All the tack, from the saddles to the boots to the bits and the bridles, were polished to perfection. Yet, it was the top hats and tailcoats that were truly striking. The top hats would shift from bobbing up and down during posting trot to gliding across the field diagonally during an extended canter maneuver. Yes, it looked like a sport for the rich. And the look of the field on that November morning left no doubt.

The sport is also peculiar in other ways. It is the only Olympic sport where women and men compete equally. There is no accommodation made for size, weight, or strength. In this sport, there is no great advantage in being young. In fact, in no other Olympic sport does experience play such a substantial role, with the average age being 37 and a couple of Olympic medalists being well into their 60s.

That early November morning, I was at the biggest event of my life. I was 23 years old, and I was up against some fantastic world-class riders, many of whom were male and were, without a doubt, physically stronger and had more years of experience. Plus, they had the benefit of recognition, having brands like Dupont and Firestone as their family name! Not to mention the financial and contact resources to acquire the best horses in the world.

Just then, I heard that whistle of his. He whistled like a horny sailor. It bothered me so much. My discomfort was likely amplified because I thought him to be a rather classy man. After all, he had wined and dined with royalty. He entertained and kept company with the richest families from America and beyond, and to me, he seemed to be quite worldly, coming from France. On that cool morning in mid-November, he used that whistle to summon me. I trotted up as I normally did and halted to a stop in front of him.

"Good morning, Jack," I said while setting my shoulders square and pressing my heels down.

"Is that so?" he said as he took a long drag of his cigarette.

Jack was wearing his typical get-up; his partridge raincoat, and pea cap. Known to be the molder of equestrian champions, he was the most successful coach of eventing riders in the world. Tough as nails, he had served in the French army and competed in the Olympics before he moved on to coach the US team. During his tenure there, his riders won 18 international medals, including several Olympic golds. No one questioned his authority when it came to horses and riders. Now, he was the head coach for the Canadian Equestrian three-day team. Rumors had it that the only reason Canada could afford him now was because he had upset some very influential American rider (or her husband!), and they ousted him.

He came up along my side and grabbed the side of my horse's bit, taking control. My horse's eyes remained fixed on him, knowing him well as the same guy that cracked a whip many times before. My horse could feel my change of state in this man's presence which kept my horse on alert.

"Actually, it's not. It's not 'good morning'". Then he took another long drag of his cigarette.

"But it could be." Jack continued.

I kept listening, hoping I could quickly figure out what in the world he was talking about. I needed to get back to my warmup routine. But I didn't have to give it much thought because he then spelled it out clearly.

He spoke slowly and quietly, straight at me in his deep, accented voice.

"You, listen to me. Look around. Look who is here. Look who you are up against."

But why was he saying this? Why was he trying to freak me out? I already knew I was a nobody in this field. My confidence was already at an all-time low. I was trying to stay out of everyone's way, out of sight of everyone warming up. I was trying to stick to a small corner in the back of the field. I did not want to bring attention to me even being there.

He continued:

"You are a nobody here. Your name is unknown. Your horse is small, and he is quite simple. And to be honest, you are not riding that well this morning."

He took another drag of his cigarette.

I'm thinking, "Oh my god. How much longer will he continue? How much longer until he excuses me to get back to my warmup routine?!"

He went on, but now, his voice had changed to a high pitch mocking tone.

"So, you can keep doing what you are doing, over in that little corner, like a little girl, and you won't bother anyone. You will go in the ring to do your little dressage test, and you will do 'okaaay". He always said OKAY like that to express how bored he was.

He paused, and his voice returned to seemingly normal. He had no more cigarettes left.

"The judges won't really take notice of you because they are tired. They are jetlagged, having flown in from around the world. Plus, two of them are hungover, and I know that for certain because I was with them last night." He made a small giggle.

I'm thinking – could he please hurry up! I've got only 14 minutes left to warm up, and my warmup routine is being completely shrugged off at my biggest and most important event!

He continued:

"You keep it up, and you will end up getting your 5s, 6s, and maybe a 7 if you are lucky. You'll come out of the ring, exhale, and that will be that. You may even be happy because it is over."

"OR," his voice changed to almost spewing disgust as he pulled down hard on my horse's bit, causing my horse to pull back and glare down.

"You can Go for it. You can stop being that little girl in that corner and start riding this field. Look up and out of your little 20-meter circle. Ride up, ride forward – give your horse some might, give your horse some wings, and fly across the ring. Get attention, be seen, take the stage, take control."

Then he released my horse's bit.

Like a flip of a switch, something had happened. I looked up and realized I was the next rider to go into the ring. I had barely 4 minutes left in my warmup.

I didn't go near the little corner of the field again. I started working in the middle. I did extended trots across the diagonal, screaming "head's up" so that no one would be in my way.

I did halts and backups and then canter forwards. I also did my half passes, shoulder-ins, and all the tough moves – in front of everyone. I was serious with my horse. I made mistakes along the way, but there were moments of brilliance. There was energy, gravitas, and attention coming my way. But I didn't care. I had an Outcome in mind.

Suddenly, I heard the bell. It was my turn to go into the ring. I kept it going. I kept the energy, focus, and attitude. As I turned the last corner, positioning myself to enter the ring and trot down the center-line, I thought to myself, this is MY moment. I eyeballed each one of those international FEI judges, and I whispered, "wake up, you mother fuckers – here I come!" I don't think anyone of them heard me, but something had registered.

It was different. The judges were the same judges. I was on the same horse and in the same arena. But the judges were now watching me, listening to me, paying attention to me. My horse was on high alert, listening to me, picking up everything. He had fancier steps, higher carriage, and pride in his eyes. And I, I was empowered. Not that I would necessarily be riskier, but I had that option. I gave myself the choices; it was up to me. I was in control. I was in process control of this massive influencing event.

What was different? What made everything different? What was it? The judges' opinion of me was different? If so, why? My horse was different, I was different. Why? This was all because of a certain mindset shift.

I finished my dressage test, gave my horse a loose rein and a big pat, and started walking out of the arena. It felt so great, and I was so happy I had to fight back the tears. I was sorry it was over, and I just wanted to do it again so I could relive the moments.

Then I heard his whistle again. The demoralizing whistle. And everything became as it were before. The switch had flipped back. Nothing had changed.

Years later, something similar happened but in a boardroom this time. I was told by an Australian male colleague that to achieve the Outcome we were after, I needed to "grow a pair." I took this to mean I needed to be tougher, more aggressive, more alpha male. I did as he suggested. I brought on a tough adversarial style to the negotiation, and we achieved our sought-after Outcome. But as I reflected on the day's event during a post negotiation audit, I realized that while we achieved our preferred Outcome, it was not the best possible Outcome. I did what I was told to do and in so doing we lost value. Something really bothered me, but I couldn't put my finger on it.

This book pinpoints exactly what went on. Exactly what transpired. We identify it, diagnose it so we can tap into it, and use it when the need arises.

W.I.N applies the principal importance of tapping into the power within and challenges the status quo. W.I.N promotes sustainable change, and achieving sustainable change requires the power trigger to come from within, from your internal resources, from your authentic self. Not from external forces and not because someone else pushed you to it.

This book and the W.I.N approach to negotiation will help you identify your strengths and channel them into having successful negotiations. In the negotiation world that often worships the alpha-male style, this book will help every woman discover her power and learn how to use her innate abilities to W.I.N in a negotiation scenario.

W.I.N is Born

FOR THE PAST 15 years, in my work as a Professional Negotiator, I've essentially helped individuals and teams get their desired Outcome.

I do this by bringing the human side into conversations. I use tools, techniques, models, and frameworks grounded in research and theory and born from behavioral science and psychology. Some of my works consider the applications of neuroscience and biochemistry. In short, the focus is on the human dynamics that take place during negotiations: the People part of the influencing act.

As a negotiator, Governments, Departments of Defense, and International Trade departments hire me to help them with large capital procurement projects and key influencing events. High-profile NGOs hire me to help them navigate through webs of complex stakeholders. International Trade departments get me involved when groups at the table have seemingly unsolvable and conflicting objectives.

I'm also hired by large multinationals in the mining/energy sector. Some of these groups asked for help negotiating the terms and conditions surrounding the clean-up of their legacy mining sites with government agencies, like the US EPA (Environmental Protection Agency). After all, who willingly wants to put their toys away and clean up their mess without trying to get out of it first!

Sometimes, I'm hired to build a plan that would help an organization improve its relationship with its suppliers for maximum gain. Or prepare individuals and teams for negotiations with unions or groups on their collective agreements. Or deal with indigenous groups for land access.

These are BIG negotiations with high stakes in very male-dominated industries.

As a woman, I'm regularly a minority in the room, even though I play a big role in developing, sculpting, and leading the strategy of the negotiation. Many times, I've been the only woman in the room and the only one leading the negotiation strategy with a team of men who are subject matter experts.

A few years back, my clientele noticeably started to shift. Venture Capitals and various finance firms started reaching out to me. The mandate was simple: prepare the teams to buy a company. However, the unsaid objective was more complex: rake the Other Party over the coals to get the best price but let the Outcome be such that the founders, the counterparties who had just been raked over the coals, will be happy to work their butts off for the next 5 or so years, for the new owners!

Large pharmaceutical clients engaged me to help them prepare for negotiations to seek WHO approvals or funding from UNITAID and such. Some other pharmaceuticals called me to work on market access negotiations. I also worked with Global Public Health teams from around the world, focused on influencing "boots on the ground" groups, high-profile NGOs, and vocal activists.

As the industries engaging in negotiation strategy and process development started to expand beyond defense, mining, and energy sectors, it became impossible to overlook the increasing number of women involved in the negotiation process. Markedly, we saw more women in the negotiating room and at the tables.

It became really interesting when Big Tech clients started to bring me in. It was a realization that the approach of lawyering up when negotiations are going 'south' could only take us so far and that a pivot in the plan could be exactly what is needed. Instead of matching the Other Party's lawyers and subject matter experts' tit for tat, why not include human behaviorists at the table? Try something else - bring behavioral science into the boardroom.

However, not all my technology clients are the big guys. I started working with small tech companies and startups to help them raise money. It was when I was working with women founders and the Women in Tech program in Palo Alto that the seed for this book was sown, and W.I.N was born.

This was the same time the Me-Too movement and Times Up movement were gaining traction. Plus, California had just legislated the 'Women on Boards' bill, which mandated every publicly held company in California to appoint at least one woman to its board on or before the stated deadline. Companies started racing to prepare women for the board seat, and many organizations started ramping up tutor efforts to help executive women handle their new board seats.

All the while, I was working with technology startups and the women founders to prepare them for negotiating equity and deal terms in the very male-dominated Venture Capital market. To fully appreciate the dynamics of these meetings, we need to consider that the guys on the other side (and I use the word guys intentionally as this small, concentrated group of financiers is very male) spend most of their day in the negotiation play. They see/hear thousands of pitches a year. Contrarily, these women founders have spent most of the last 5-10 years building the businesses they were about to pitch. One can't compare the negotiation experience or the pitch practice between these two sides.

During these work sessions, it felt like we were preparing to negotiate away our baby. We spoke a lot about strategies to shift the perception of the power balance to not feel like the smaller person in the room. We worked on tactics to sound stronger and tougher. We worked on using the time variable for pace control. We also worked on increasing our gravitas with our body language and tone.

While working with the women founders and Women in Tech groups for fundraising negotiations, we worked tirelessly on ways to alter the power balance perception in the pitch room. We worked on; *"Fake It till You Make It"* strategies, ways to Be Big, take up MORE space, take up MORE room, have a louder voice, a larger presence, more gravitas. Get more respect! Basically, how to negotiate successfully as a woman in this male-dominated world.

Guess what? It worked. For short periods of time, after we worked very hard, we would take the stage and create a psychological atmosphere that allowed us to feel like we were in power. With a lot of work, we could be in process control of the negotiation for a short period of time.

Even though we were recording good successes with this approach, I wasn't completely happy. Sure, we were talking with more confidence. We were successful in avoiding being brushed off. We were getting more attention. But something was missing from our plan. Something bothered me.

"*Fake It till You Make It*" is exhausting! Working outside your reflex zone is tiring. While we spent time working on our body language and tone, the Other Party spent their time researching the content of the negotiation. While we practiced tactics to avoid rescinding to intimidation, the Other Party spent their time developing alternatives, ultimately giving them real power. We were splitting our time and resources into areas the Other Party didn't even have to consider. We were working hard just to play on their field.

There had to be a better way. A more equal way. Why should we have to deal with a handicap in the first place? How can we not deal with a handicap? What are the ways to eliminate this handicap altogether?

I delved deep into this question and started to interview female senior executives and negotiators from around the world. From different backgrounds, capacities, and industries, the conversations were remarkably the same; fascinating, enlightening, and reaffirming. Insights were gathered, and assumptions were tested.

One time, I was speaking with a big tech corporate council executive and her business leader counterpart with whom I had worked. The conversation shifted to the importance of being authentic. The value of not trying to be something or someone you are not. The importance and benefits of being our unique selves. Not having the burden of needing to 'do it their way, or a certain way' but rather, the license to do it **my way**. With the caveat that, of course, it must be done and done well. I took that notion to another conversation where we spoke about empowerment and concluded that nothing is more empowering than realizing that being yourself is the best play to make. After all, who can be better at being you than you?

Women in Negotiation (W.I.N) and this book continued to form in my mind throughout the duration of these conversations. A few months later, while in a work group session with the Program on Negotiation with the Harvard Law school I had an epiphany. It was during a Kelman Series seminar on international conflict hosted by Harvard University. There was discussion around how to negotiate with a tough guy; Putin was the example. We looked at how to humanize the Other Party, diagnose personal drivers, identify their personal needs, and diffuse 'red' or 'hot' interactions. It was a fantastic presentation and brought to light the importance of understanding the Other Party's psychological realities if we want to drive behavioral change.

Part of the discussion was about Putin's heroes being KGB agents/spies. To bring this point to life, the presenter included a slide that showcased James Bond and the very sexy Bond girl.

We also discussed the experiences/moments in Putin's life that shaped his perspectives. One of such moments was said to be his mother's sufferings during the Soviet era. The presentation spoke about the fact that Putin's mother had practically starved herself because she gave her food rations to her husband so he would have the strength to carry on and work. To buttress the point, there was a picture in the slide deck of a starving, frail-looking elderly woman.

The presentation was strong and included great arguments. The presentation deck was powerful, but of course, it did not portray women as smart or strong. As, of course, that was not the point. In fact, the point was the opposite.

Yet, regardless of whether this was the point or not, the chat boxes just went crazy after these slides were shown and for the rest of the forum. Participants were going nuts. Women who were participating in the workshop were losing it.

"This is wrong! We are talking about Negotiation. Women need to be portrayed properly."

"How dare you, during a topic on negotiation, portray women as BOND models or starving weak mothers."

"Where are the pictures of the strong women?"

"How can we include more women?"

"What about more seats at the table for women?"

I've been in negotiations where I was the only woman at the table. During my interviews with top women executives and women negotiators, it was evident that they, too, had experienced being the minority at the table. Donna Hicks, who leads the Kelman Seminar series and authored the book 'Dignity,' was also present at the forum, and later, she shared with me she, too, had experienced being the only female in the negotiating room. Women being solo in a negotiation was not new. I understood the frustration that was being channeled through the chat boxes as comments. I knew what they meant, and I knew how they felt, but the way the messages were sent, and the tone in which they were sent, wasn't working. It was not showcasing our strengths as negotiator. Rather, it came across as bitter and angry.

Then I had an epiphany - we are going at this the wrong way. We need to tackle women in negotiations from a different angle. Flip it, make it positive, and empowering.

W.I.N flips the approach. Instead of working to be something we are not, W.I.N drives us to own our characteristics and use them to our benefit. It does not only give you the "license to be you," but also the realization that being our authentic selves is the most powerful performance.

There is indisputable uniqueness in every woman. In fact, in every individual. Our individual set of characteristics is what makes us, us. So, how do we take that uniqueness and make it work to our advantage?

Instead of changing, don't change. Own it, and make it work. Instead of being mad because we are not being accommodated, we can make the lack of accommodation work to our benefit.

Flip it, make it positive, and empowering, take control. Don't try to be something you are not but take what you are and use it to its fullest.

For example:

For the most part, women are smaller, lighter, less hairy, and less scary... Could this be an advantage?

I've worked with clients to increase their presence, take up more space and more air. This could be a good angle, and of course, it's an option. But then, why can't we use this natural uniqueness as an asset? Instead of changing, can we use what we have now as an asset to succeed at the negotiation table?

For the most part, women have a greater ability to appreciate the needs of others. This stems from neurological and biochemical differences, which we will touch on later in this book.

Often, we are told, *"don't let them bully you." "Stand up for yourself." "Get what you deserve."* But we are not weak, neither are we running from a fight. Many of our actions come from understanding the needs of others, and we can use this instinct of understanding others as a great asset in a negotiation that is on its way to a deadlock.

As women, we are sometimes told not to take things personally. We hear words like *"you are too sensitive," "don't have such thin skin,"* and so on. So, instead of trying to 'grow a pair' which is not easy, and personally, I don't wish to do, what about taking our sensitivity – our over-sensitive, thin skin and using it as an asset?

Over the course of the interviews I had with the women executives, the conversations circled around 5 key characteristics that women exhibit. I realized that when you superimpose these female characteristics against 5 key Negotiation Bedrock Concepts, it is remarkable to note that women have a distinct advantage to win in the negotiation arena.

W.I.N examines 5 key Negotiation Bedrock Concepts, the characteristics of skilled negotiators with respect to these concepts, and how they line up with women's negotiation superpowers: The Female Five!

At the end of the day, we don't have to fight to WIN. And our greatest asset is ourselves.

Key Bedrock Negotiation Concepts & The Female Five

BEDROCK CONCEPT 1

SKILLED NEGOTIATORS MASTER
DUAL COMPETENCIES
The What & The How
MANAGE IN PARALLEL

BEDROCK CONCEPT 2

SKILLED NEGOTIATORS
know
the underpinning skillsets for:

Negotiating
and
Influencing
are identical

use these skills to
Shape
PERCEPTIONS

BEDROCK CONCEPT 3

SKILLED NEGOTIATIATORS
Diagnose
P.I.N. ICEBERG

BEDROCK CONCEPT 4

SKILLED NEGOTIATIATORS
are aware of:
Psychological Reactance
and use to create and claim value

TELL

ASK

What do you want?
Which one do you choose?
What do you think?

BEDROCK CONCEPT 5

Skilled Negotiators know

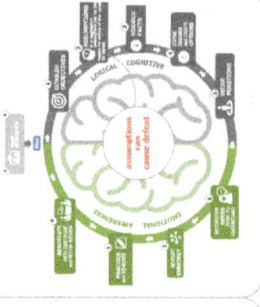

Multitasking   Intuition   Empathy   Humility   Physical

It's Time to Cash In.

You are driving a dually truck down Interstate 95 in the middle of traffic, pulling a horse trailer with two horses in the back. With your lunch on your lap, you glance in the rear-view mirror at intervals to put on mascara while on a hands-free call, negotiating a refund of a pair of riding gloves that arrived late.

You have the innate ability to multitask!

Negotiation Bedrock Concept 1

THERE IS ONE key characteristic that separates skilled negotiators from the rest. In this key bedrock trait, women are great because of their ability to multitask.

Women's ability to process information quickly and carry out tasks simultaneously is almost supernatural. This type of simultaneous, sensory & mental multitasking is exactly what is needed to master the dual negotiation competencies and manage them concurrently, in parallel.

Negotiations are comprised of two main components, and skilled Negotiators can clearly distinguish between the two, master the competencies required for each, and manage the two components in parallel. This could be ultra-demanding when we consider that each of the competencies is so dissimilar and require different talents. So, what are these two components of a negotiation?

The WHAT – The Substance of the Negotiation

The first component of a negotiation is the SUBSTANCE of the negotiation. The Content of the negotiation, the WHAT we will be negotiating. Unarguably a vital part of the negotiation, for there would be no need to negotiate if there was nothing to negotiate.

As skilled negotiators, we need to clearly know the content of the negotiation in all its parts. We need to know this content so intricately that we can split it into pieces and different categories while keeping its value intact. We then need to know how to squeeze out more value from these different forms, clearly and concisely adding options, expanding the pie, and sculpting out intricate creative values and solutions.

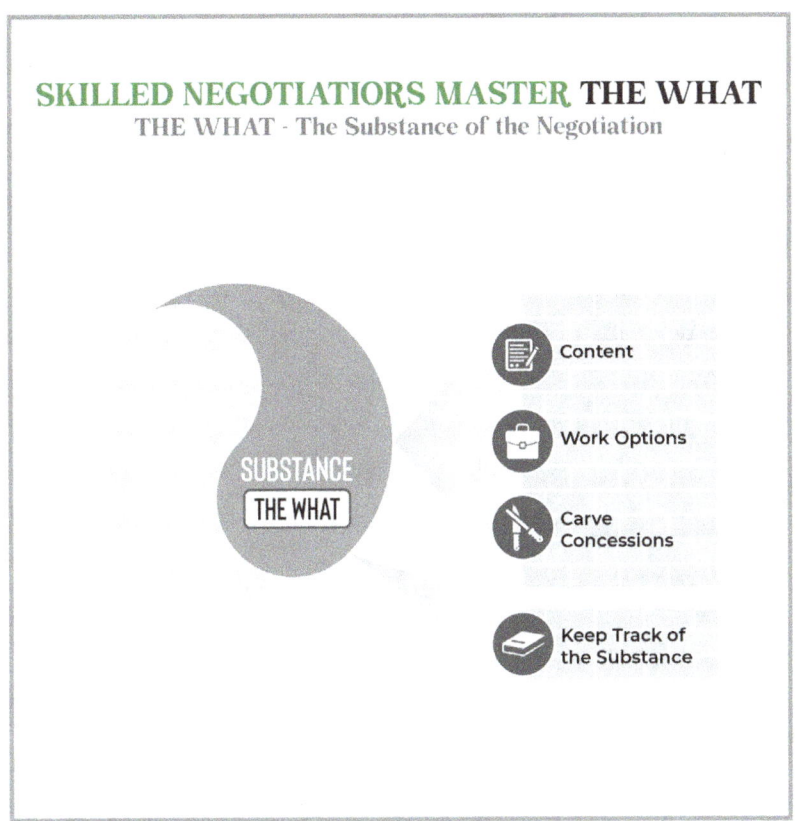

This competency requires detailed thinking and analytical critiquing. It relies heavily on the left brain for analytical interpretation of information and logical application to measure value and returns. Skilled negotiators know how to surgically carve out pieces of value and blocks of content and then serve them up to the Other Party as value trades and concessions.

This is not simple stuff, even for those who really know their stuff. Sometimes, knowing the subject matter so expertly can be a disadvantage, and herein lies The Great Paradox of this complex social process we call a negotiation.

"Experts in their field" often zoom in on the substance and the details. They are naturally attracted to that part. They are comfortable with the content. This is particularly true for those who really know their stuff and, in my experience, especially true for scientists, engineers, and members of the legal profession. These mavens are trained to look expertly at the content. Either when designing a system or finding a loophole in the contract, they are always comfortable deep in the details. Entrepreneurs also have this knack. Entrepreneurs can be so attached to their business, their baby, that it can be hard to fathom how anything else can be more important to them, especially when the negotiation is about their business.

And this leads us to the second component of negotiation

– THE HOW

The HOW – The Process of the Negotiation

If the first component is the WHAT of the negotiation, then the second component is the HOW. It's one thing to know WHAT you want, but it's quite another to know how to get it. How are we going to get this done? How will we get what we want? This is often referred to as the People part of the negotiation. The human part. The Substance part of the negotiation requires us to understand what is at stake and on the table, while the second component, the Process part of the negotiation, requires us to understand what is going on around the table and in the room!

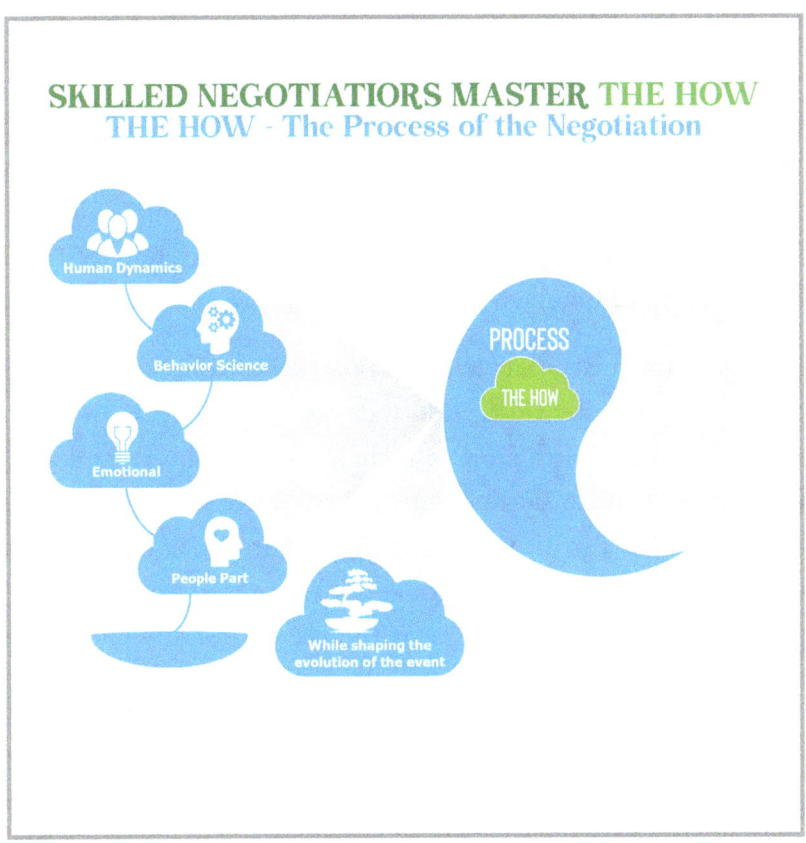

This competency requires high emotional intelligence, intuition, and social skills. With our right brain leading, we need to know what the Other Party is saying with their eyes while their mouth says something else. We need to know who really calls the shots and who is unaware of this. We need to understand when to discuss a difficult matter or when to quickly change the subject. We need to know how we will get things done, have a plan for the process, and be in control of driving the plan forward.

DUAL COMPETENCIES MANAGED IN PARALLEL

The two negotiation components are different and should be distinguished, yet they happen concurrently and need to be managed simultaneously, in parallel. Noting how different the competencies are, it is tough and exhausting to work them simultaneously. It requires all facets of our intelligence, Emotional Quotient (EQ) and Intelligence Quotient (IQ), to be 'switched on.'

Managing the dual competencies in parallel requires us to analyze the value of the offer to our side and their side, while leaning into a hunch that it's worth more to them than it is to us, regardless of what was presented. Or uncovering the creative solution that will solve the Other Party's problem as well as our own and then crafting the dialogue so that the idea appears to sprout from their side to make compliance easy. We need to see the forest while seeing the trees. It requires us to act on stage while watching the action from the balcony and then react again based on what we've seen. It requires **Simultaneous, Sensory & Mental Multitasking**.

We need to see the forest while seeing the trees.

It requires **Simultaneous, Sensory & Mental Multitasking**.

But wait, there's more! Master negotiators are skilled at mixing up these dual competencies. We need to bring the left brain to the right brain and the right brain to the left to add creativity to the content and come up with new ideas and creative solutions and then add order to the chaos, structure to our process and framing to our feelings.

This is multitasking at its best; simultaneous, sensory, and mental multitasking. And women are hard-wired for it!

WOMEN and Multitasking

Multitasking refers to the performance of a variety of tasks at the same time. Originally defined by researchers and psychologists, multitasking is considered a broad concept in the field of psychology and has been developed and over developed for years.

There are at least three types of multitasking:

1. Consecutive Mental Multitasking

The first type is the skill associated with the ability to deal with the demands of multiple tasks without actually performing those tasks simultaneously. For example, being able to jump off one task to complete another and then return to the first. It's called Consecutive Mental Multitasking, and research shows that it takes us, on average, 8 minutes to get back on track with the first task after taking a break. Regardless, easy peasy!

2. Simultaneous Multitasking

The second type of multitasking requires you to simultaneously process and carry out two or more types of information. This type is called Simultaneous Multitasking. Think about focusing on a work project on a conference call while keeping a kid engaged on an activity and re-hammering a nail into the wall to level a painting you noticed was hanging crooked. All at the same time!

3. Sensory Multitasking

There is a third type of multitasking, and it is called Sensory Multitasking. It is the ability to process different types of sensory information at the same time. For example, processing what you hear someone say with their voice versus what you see them say with their eyes at the same time. Or hearing someone say yes and picking up in the tone that it is a 'no.' Sensory multitasking is when you can pick up and process sets of information coming at you from your different senses. You do it quickly, distinctly, and simultaneously.

The combination of all three types of multitasking is required for a successful negotiation: Simultaneous, Mental, and Sensory Multitasking. In this combination type, women can do and do well.

It remains a mystery as no one knows exactly why women prevail in multitasking. Were women trained to be this way, or does it come naturally?

OR

On the one hand, society has trained women to multitask. For years, societal pressures have had us doing so many things at the same time. The COVID pandemic stay-at-home orders, online school for children, and work from home for adults commanded even more of this skill. Often, we are given, sometimes by ourselves, accolades for being able to do it all. Whether it is good for us or not is another point entirely.

On the other hand, perhaps it's due to an evolutionary twist. There is an extrapolation of the Hunter-Gatherer hypothesis[1] that states that the cognitive adaptation of women's role as gatherers (versus men as hunters) required the use of multiple facets of the brain at the same time. Looking over the family and children while doing the chores and gathering food called for great multitasking skills, compared to hunting that requires a total streamlined focus.

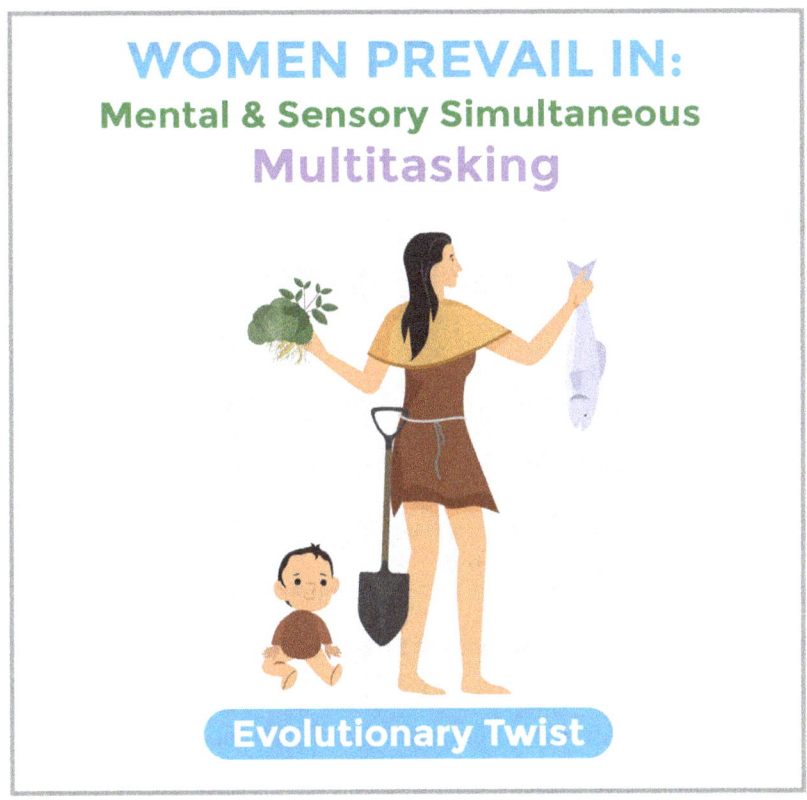

Or is the capacity to do a number of things at the same time just part of our biology? Our makeup? Our uniqueness? The most basic yet absolute and indisputable proof is the truth that women build a baby while going on with their daily activities.

Regardless of the reason, self-trained or simply a social requirement, women are better at using multiple facets of their brains and parts of the body at the same time. Right or wrong, for good or bad, women have, for a very long time, managed a million things on the go, usually performing several tasks at the same time. We've practiced and practiced and now perfected this ability. It is now time for us to cash in on this uniquely female talent in the negotiation milieu.

The ability to use both sides of the brain, your Intelligence Quotient (IQ) and Emotional Quotient (EQ), at the same time is what is known as Simultaneous, Sensory & Mental Multitasking, and that's exactly what we need to master the dual competencies required in a negotiation and to manage them in parallel. The sky's the limit for negotiators who excel in mastering these competencies simultaneously.

Chapter 1 Summary

There are two distinct components in a negotiation:

1. The Substance - The What
2. The Process - The How

Skilled negotiators are aware of the two components and can clearly distinguish between the two. Both the Substance and the Process of the negotiation develop concurrently, and a skilled negotiator must manage/control both simultaneously. This is called Simultaneous, Sensory & Mental Multitasking. In this key negotiation trait, women are great!

Right or wrong, women have been juggling many things and wearing different hats for years. Practiced and perfected, women's ability to process information quickly and carry out tasks simultaneously is now almost supernatural. This type of multitasking is exactly what is needed to master the complex dual negotiation competencies, distinguish them from each other and manage them in parallel.

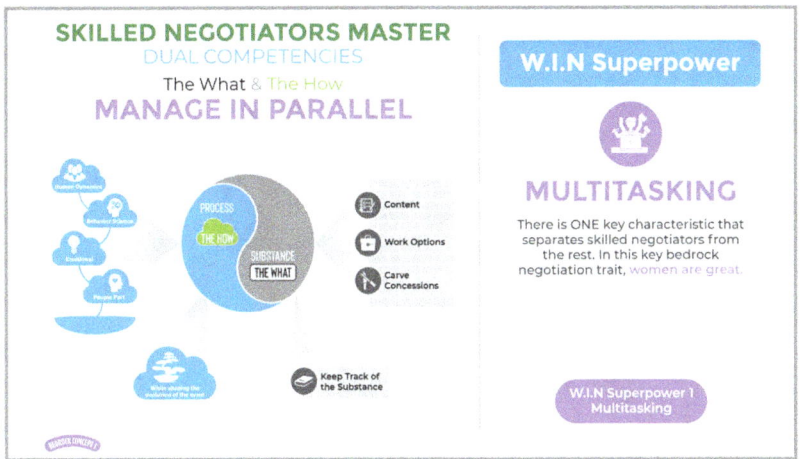

Negotiation Tip!

The Male Mud Tactic.
When the Counterparty (CP) finds comfort in focusing on the substance, the content, and details of the negotiation, a useful tactic can be to send them down to the details of the deal and get them caught in the Male Mud- their own Content Quicksand. This allows you to jump into your **"Process drone"** and control the negotiation process from way up there!

The Extra Antenna

You are now two hours out of the traffic and cruising down the highway. For no apparent reason, you pull over to the right outside lane and slow down a little. The highway dips slightly, you go around a bend, and there he is. A highway patroller hiding in the bushes with the radar speed gun pointed your way.

It was your extra antenna – your Woman's intuition.

You subconsciously noticed that the cars on the other lane were moving slower than the cars a mile back. Cars in the other lane were not passing one another – everyone driving prudently. You subconsciously recorded that the bend in the highway had speed traps on the other side. The slight hill would trap people into going over the speed limit. It was a sunny warm day and a nice environment for a police officer to sit and watch.

These are the aggregate of nuances that got recorded in our subconscious.

Negotiation Bedrock Concept 2

NEGOTIATION IS A complex social process filled with uncertainty and ambiguity, with so much happening outside our conscious awareness. This is why the second Negotiation Bedrock Concept is so important. This bedrock concept can be explained as two sides of the same coin. On one side, we pick up on internal and external cues that shape OUR mindset and perceptions, and on the other side, we must manage the development of the Other Party's beliefs. Successfully executing this concept requires a keen evaluation and quick analysis of our gut instincts. The well-known and ever-present Women's **Intuition** is our distinct advantage in this critical skillset

What is my intuition picking up? How is that shaping what I believe? What's my hunch?

Uncertainty and ambiguity are unavoidable during a negotiation. But this uncertainty and ambiguity provide us with the possibility to frame and revise perceptions. What message am I sending out to the Other Party? How is that shaping their mindset? What has it impressed upon them? What displeases them? Huge questions, and this is where our intuition comes to the rescue.

Let's look at a few fun scenarios to bring our Negotiation Bedrock Concept 2 to life:

Scenario A - yucky

You are a mother serving dinner to her two children. You notice that your 10-year-old is eating all their vegetables while your 6-year-old is not. In fact, they are clowning around and being a bit wasteful with the food.

You say to your 10-year-old: "Wow! You are doing a great job with your veggies. You are going to be so strong. And thank you for being polite."

- Is there a negotiation taking place?

- If so, then who are the parties in the negotiation?

In this scenario, is there a negotiation taking place? Is there an outcome being sought? Who are the parties to this negotiation? Who is being influenced and by whom?

In this example, the younger child who is not eating their vegetables is likely influenced by the dialogue between the mother and the older child. Whether this is orchestrated or not, the fact that the conversation is taking place "beside" her in no way makes the message less powerful. Her mindset is altered as she hears the mother praise the other child for eating her veggies.

Let's have a look at another scenario:

Scenario B - pizza?

You are a hostage negotiator brought to the scene to negotiate the release of 11 captive children. The high-level task force greets you as you arrive.

They watch on as you make the following first exchange with the hostage taker:

"Hi, I'm (your name), I'm going to pull out my ID. Now, before we do anything, let's get comfortable. I'm going to order some pizza. What do you like on your pizza?"

· Is there a negotiation taking place?

· If so, then who are the parties in the negotiation?

This is a classic hostage negotiation scenario with a captor and negotiator. Let's zoom in to the moment where the parties first start to talk. Is that moment part of the negotiation? Are mindsets being prepped at that moment? Are perceptions being formed? Is there an outcome being sought? Who are the parties to this negotiation? Who is being influenced by whom?

In this example, there are at least two negotiations taking place. The first and most central to the focus is the interchange between the hostage-taker and the negotiator.

Now, let's dive deep into the details of this exchange to unpack what is taking place:

"Hi, I'm Susie..." Here, we immediately get personal with a name, which is often the very first sentence and the very first piece of information we give the Other Party. This helps the Other Party to see us as a human. It is the most fundamental and indisputable piece of early common ground. With these three words, we are

also 'giving something' to the Other Party. We are giving them information, our name in this instance. We are massaging their subconscious with the notion that we are open; we have given, and they have already received from us. At this moment in their mind, they are winning.

"Before we do anything, let's get comfortable...." This is mainly to build process and personal Common Ground. Using "we" and "let's" suggests the same side advantage. It makes the Other Party feel you are both on the same side.

"I'm going to order some pizza. What do you like on your pizza?" The pizza offer is the negotiation tactic known as "Inoculation." The Inoculation negotiation tactic is when we inject something along the way that we can use to our advantage later. Here, we inoculate a "give" for a potential future "ask." For example: "Remember, I brought you pizza, so you owe me X."

"What do you like on your pizza?" This low-risk open-ended question adds some value to our inoculation tactic: "Not only did I bring you pizza, but I also got you what you liked, pineapple on your pizza. Now you really owe me...."

Asking the question, the beautiful question, also achieves a few other interesting things for you:

a. You find out something. This helps us to build a profile of the Other Party. All information about the Other Party, the case, content, or the situation is beneficial. We never know what pieces of information will surface later and how they may help us build our strategy.

b. By asking a question, you allow the Other Party to TELL you what they want. By telling us, they psychologically believe they have the upper hand and know more than us. When we agree, in this case, to pineapple on the pizza, they get additional something from us. In this case, pineapple on the pizza is the something, and is of absolutely no value to us. Yet, it adds to the Other Party's misconception that they are in charge, we've given, and they are winning.

c. By asking a question, we get the Other Party to communicate. This allows us to capture a ton of information and mentally register the following: their chosen channel, did they answer themselves verbally, did they get another to answer on their behalf, did they send written word, what words did they choose, what was the tone, what was the accent and on and on. Even a no answer or silence will give us information we can use.

With all this information, we start to build a picture and shape our beliefs. We build the baseline for their behavior, and style (word choice, voice, and tempo) that all subsequent communications will be judged against. This will be our compass to where their emotions are going during the negotiation interactions.

On the flipside, during this small interaction, you are also planting the baseline you want them to use for you. You are setting how you want them to "see" you for the duration of the negotiation.

The second, less obvious negotiation in this scenario is between the hostage negotiator and the high-level task force. Like the first scenario we looked at, side talks and concurrent events have a high capacity to influence. We must always be aware of how we are influenced by interactions around us and how we influence those watching our interactions. In this case, the members of the high-level task force, likely unaware, are being influenced by your demeanor. And they, in turn, are shaping their perceptions of you.

In the final scenario, Scenario C, let's bring it back to the business world.

Scenario C- elevator pitch

You are a CEO of a global Fortune 500, and you (with your team) just pitched your Board of Directors the idea to acquire a competitor. Your presentation lasts 30 minutes and you feel you did a very good job.

As you and your team get in the elevator to go down to the main floor, the Chairman of the Board rushes to get in the elevator. He is the boss! In essence, he controls the Board's decision.

In the elevator, while looking forward at the door, he says loudly for all to hear:

"That was a good presentation, I'd like to see more of those."

- Is there a negotiation taking place?
- if so, then who are the parties in the negotiation?

In this scenario, have you been influenced? Did the ambiguity of the Chairman's actions shape a perception? You might be thinking, what does he mean? Was the message directed at me? Or is the message to one of the team members? It is highly unlikely, almost inevitable, that you leave the elevator without being affected by the chairman's actions.

These three scenarios illustrate our Negotiation Bedrock Concept 2:

Negotiating, influencing, convincing, manipulating, persuading… all do the job of moving parties to an Outcome. Mindsets are prepped, and perceptions are shaped at orchestrated and unorchestrated events, away from the table.

Negotiation Bedrock Concept 2

SKILLED NEGOTIATIORS

know
the underpinning skillsets for:

Negotiating

and

Influencing

are identical

use these skills to

Shape

PERCEPTIONS

BEDROCK CONCEPT 2

Skilled negotiators ascertain and shape perceptions through actions taken at and away from the negotiating table. This requires wide lens awareness of what is going on…on both sides!

External cues coming from the Other Side:

We must be able to read the room and pick up the clues coming from the Other Party:

Why did he rush to get in the elevator with us? It is jam-packed.

Why did they give each other a glance?

Why are the suit jackets buttoned up when the room is hot?

What are they not telling me?

Their face has changed color!

The hands are now locked.

The tempo has picked up!

Internal cues we can pick up:

We must be keenly aware of the internal cues we are receiving. What is our body telling us about the Other Party or the situation?

Why do I just feel good about this person?

Why does my gut tell me not to mention that incident?

My heart is racing. Why?

I don't feel good about the meeting vibe- something was up.

On their side:

At the same time, we must also be aware of the total communication cluster we send to the Other Party. What message are we passing on about ourselves, our feelings, beliefs, perceptions, and positions?

I'm passionate about a point - am I coming across as hardheaded and defensive?

When I sent the email at 7:30am, what message,
beyond the words in the email, was I sending?

I attended the meeting alone and was 7 minutes late. Message?

I brought the corporate council and technology expert
with me to the meeting, and we were early. Message?

We skipped the intro and got right down to business. Message?

Skilled negotiators understand that perceptions are shaped, and mindsets are prepped during ALL interactions, each and every event at and away from the table. The ambiguity and uncertainty in negotiations make way for this to happen. By the time formal talks start, people have built a strong position and point of view of each other.

Skilled negotiators are hyper-alert of the communications clusters they send to the Other Party. They make their best efforts to ensure all messages and channels, direct and indirect, verbal, and non-verbal, deliver the correct message – to ultimately drive towards the Outcome they want to achieve.

WOMEN and The Extra Antenna

During the life of a negotiation, picking up on the aggregate of nuances allows one to capture critical insights. From identifying stakeholder alliances to diagnosing personal triggers, women have the extra antenna!

Women are said to possess a superior intuition, an almost psychic and sometimes frightening "knack for knowing," but this inclination is often undervalued in our (male) logic-based society.

Women's intuition is a real thing and a major advantage in a nego-tiation. In fact, it can make all the difference to the negotiation Outcome in a high-stress situation. Often occurring outside of our conscious awareness, we draw on social cues, internal and exter-nal cues to make rapid, in-the-moment decisions — an imperative skill for a negotiator and particularly for high-stress negotiations. Our intuition relies on our ability to instantaneously evaluate both internal and external signals, and make a decision based on what appears to be pure instinct.

Women's Intuition – it is a real thing.

That gut feeling is way more than just a feeling. Women's Intuition is a real thing! And it is a major advantage to have on high alert during the life of a negotiation.

Some experts say women's intuition is based on their ability to read facial expressions and body language. That's true, but that's certainly not all. There is much more to the story. There are a few factors that help to explain why we have that sixth sense.

The first is that women tend to have better bilateral use of their brains. In other words, they pay more attention to the right side of their brain, which is associated with intuitive perception. One study used MRI scans to compare the male and female brain connectivity. The result discovered that the typical male brain is neurologically wired to be more logical and, thus, more effective at linking perception with action. Whereas the female brain has more neural connections going from side to side across the left and right hemispheres which makes women better at interpreting social phe-nomena, including social cues. Put simply, males are hardwired to be logical, while females are hardwired to be intuitive.

THE MALE AND FEMALE BRAIN

A new way of showing the connectivity of the brain - called "connectome" maps - reveals significant difference between men and women

Typical male brain (top view)

Most connections run between front and back parts of the same hemisphere. This could account for the better spatial skills and motor muscle control in men.

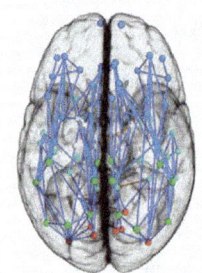

Typical female brain (top view)

Many more neural connections go from side to side across the left and right hemispheres. Scientists say this could account for women's for better verbal skills and intuitive abilities.

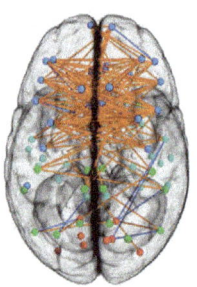

Secondly, women are brought up to be more in touch with their feelings, which allows them to be more intuitive. From an early age, women are conditioned to take the back seat, listen, and observe, which are the key steps to take to "read a room."

Another study suggests that women's heightened intuition emerged over the course of human evolution. Elaborate brain circuitry-forming instincts evolved so our forebears could quickly size up a person or a situation. Women, traditionally entrusted with looking after the young and often not having the physical advantage to fight, evolved to have stronger, more accurate instincts to better protect their offspring from any potential threats.

Chapter 2 Summary

The second key Negotiation Bedrock Concept deals with shaping perceptions at and away from the table. Skilled negotiators are aware of ALL the opportunities they have to shape mindsets and influence the Other Party.

At the same time, they are keenly aware of how and why their feelings are formed and how and why their attitudes are developed. This requires picking up on the aggregate of nuances to form an opinion. This unconscious form of reasoning, our intuition, is a valuable advantage and should be a voice we listen to during the life of a negotiation. Women's Intuition is the real thing. Women have superior intuition than men, giving us an upper hand in negotiating.

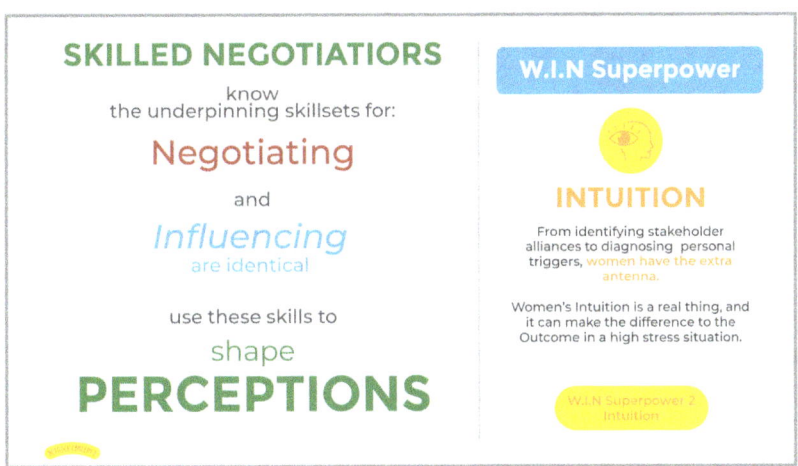

W.I.N Negotiation Superpower 2: Listen to your gut.

Women are often criticized for being too sensitive, emotional, and illogical. We are told *"don't be so sensitive," "you have to have thicker skin."* This constant barrage of criticism can cloud our judgment and make us doubt ourselves and our instincts. To the contrary!

Our thinner skin allows us to pick up clues and cues. Our sensitivity fuels our intuition. Instead of being 'not so sensitive,' we should cultivate our pure instinct and take note of insights coming from our intuition. We need to recognize our intuition as a negotiation weapon, not a liability. Let intuition have a voice in our decisions.

The little voice in the back of your mind, the feeling in your gut – it's much more than a little voice or just a feeling. It is an elaborate brain circuitry deciphering messages from your senses and combining them with your experiences. Society says to push it away, but it is your personal GPS that is available 24/7.

It is a Negotiation Superpower!

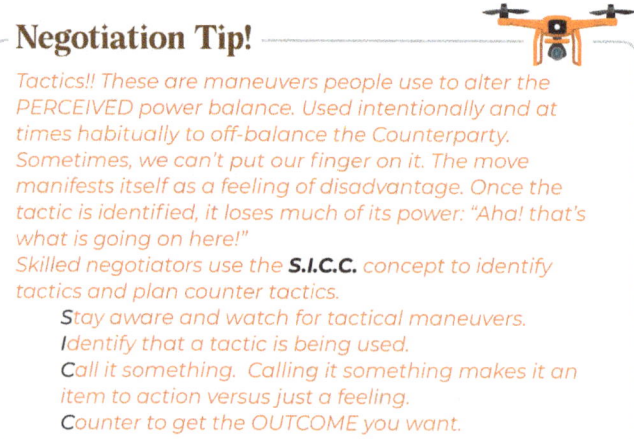

Negotiation Tip!

Tactics!! These are maneuvers people use to alter the PERCEIVED power balance. Used intentionally and at times habitually to off-balance the Counterparty. Sometimes, we can't put our finger on it. The move manifests itself as a feeling of disadvantage. Once the tactic is identified, it loses much of its power: "Aha! that's what is going on here!"
Skilled negotiators use the **S.I.C.C.** concept to identify tactics and plan counter tactics.
    Stay aware and watch for tactical maneuvers.
    Identify that a tactic is being used.
    Call it something. Calling it something makes it an item to action versus just a feeling.
    Counter to get the OUTCOME you want.

That's Their Problem!…**Not**!

The triple combination in show jumping is hands down the most challenging effort on the course. There's almost no room for error, no time for recovery, or space to play catch-up inside a sequence of three jumps spaced one or two strides apart. The key is for horse and rider to maintain agility, flexibility, coordination, and emotional control.

You practice the correct pace as you approach the first jump. You do a steady up half halt, your right inside leg for momentum and your outside leg holds the rear. You straighten up, sit close to the tack, and chin up. You can feel your horse sees the jumps, ears are perked, the pace is good, and your horse………screeches to a stop! For the 3rd time in a row.

You scream in frustration - "I don't know what your problem is!"

Bingo.

Negotiation Bedrock Concept 3

Our third bedrock concept is also the first step in the Negotiation Process. This is to diagnose the needs of the other side. In this critical step, women are rock stars!!

I'm often hired to work with a client after something has gone wrong. Brought in by CEOs because the lawyers were messing things up, or the negotiation with a supplier or customer was "going the wrong way." Sometimes the players, the personalities, are tired and annoyed.

So, I get invited and caught up on where things stand. I ask questions about the background, objectives, and parties to the negotiation. I listen as they tell me what went well (usually not so much at this point) and what didn't go so well. Within the first five minutes of the conversation (usually, the part when we are focused on all our goodwill gestures), I hear them say in one form or another:

"I don't know what their problem is!"

Herein lies the greatest negotiation myth of all time -

<u>*The Other Person's problem is solely their own*</u>.

Thinking that their problem is NOT your problem - is the problem! In a negotiation, the Other Party's problem is your problem, your concern. In a commercial negotiation, it is literally your business. The Other Party is in the negotiation for their needs, not yours. To move the negotiation forward, we must think of them, figure out their needs and work out how to solve their problem. Only then will we have the parts to create the solutions that meet their needs as well as ours.

To make things even more interesting, when looking through the lens of human behavior, one will discover the existence of several different degrees of NEEDS. The PIN (Positions – Interests – Needs) iceberg model illustrates this perfectly.

On the surface, for all to see, we have our logical, overt, stated POSITIONS. These are often tied to company financials, high ethical standards, and public personas.

Think of an upper-class British accent: "*yes, of course….*"

Just like an ocean, lake, or river, it's when we go below the surface that we often find a few surprises! As we look under the water-line, hidden below the surface, we discover the real INTERESTS behind the positions. The unstated 'why' of the positions. Often, these interests are originally unstated on purpose or for strategic reasons. At other times, the interests are not shared because they are too personal, sometimes even subconscious. For example, a stated Position could be that the deal has a deadline of December 31st. The unstated Interest behind that deadline could be the desire to hit an annual budget and a bonus!

As we go down further, we can discover deep emotions, fear-based behaviors, injustices, and ideologies. Here we find the NEEDs. This can be driven by unconscious triggers and can be powerful heavy-duty stuff.

See the example below:

A procurement professional discovered through a subordinate that their supplier offered a new competitor a better pricing structure than what was offered to this procurement professional. We can use the PIN iceberg model to identify the Positions, Interests, and Needs of this procurement professional.

On the surface, the stated Position for the procurement professional is to get a better deal. As we move into the Interest behind the position, we uncover the desire to appear good at their jobs and save face. As we dig further down, we discover the unconscious Need for respect, pride, and safeguarding one's dignity. Just like this procurement professional, we all have personal triggers that live deep within our iceberg. This is especially important to remember when working in a team- every member of the team has a P.I.N iceberg.

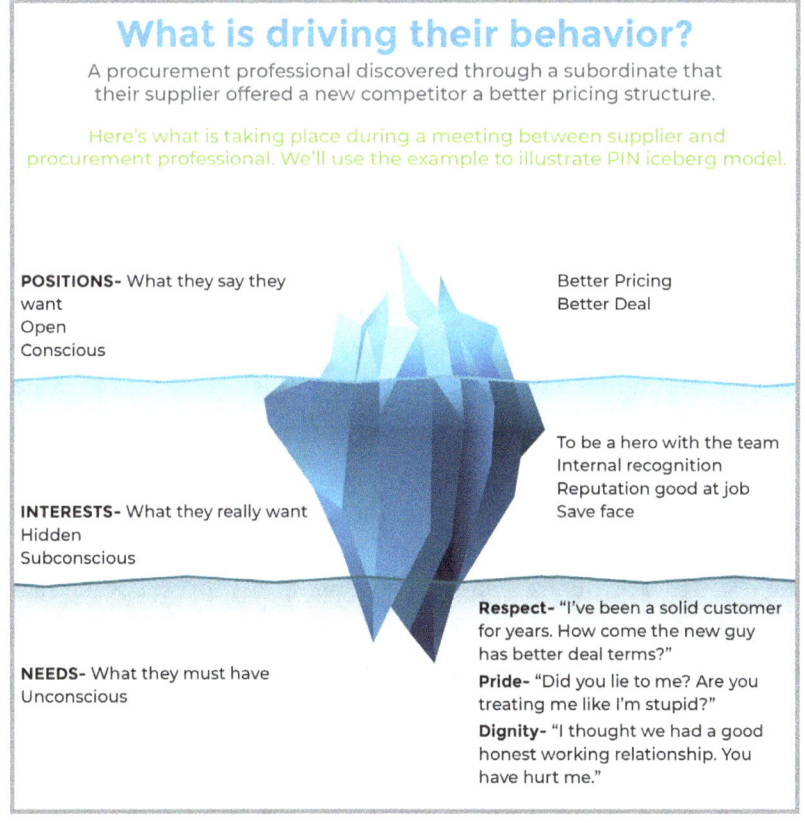

What is driving their behavior?

A procurement professional discovered through a subordinate that their supplier offered a new competitor a better pricing structure.

Here's what is taking place during a meeting between supplier and procurement professional. We'll use the example to illustrate PIN iceberg model.

POSITIONS- What they say they want
Open
Conscious

Better Pricing
Better Deal

INTERESTS- What they really want
Hidden
Subconscious

To be a hero with the team
Internal recognition
Reputation good at job
Save face

NEEDS- What they must have
Unconscious

Respect- "I've been a solid customer for years. How come the new guy has better deal terms?"

Pride- "Did you lie to me? Are you treating me like I'm stupid?"

Dignity- "I thought we had a good honest working relationship. You have hurt me."

Skilled negotiators know the importance of diagnosing the Other Party's iceberg in its entirety – on all levels. Until we can diagnose the needs of the Other Party and put our finger on what they are feeling, truly feeling, we may be unable to find a solution. In a negotiation, the Other Party's problem is our problem to solve.

To truly understand the person or people we are dealing with would require deep, authentic curiosity about their experiences. We need to be opened to experiencing the world through their eyes, knowing they could hold different, maybe even deeply, contrary positions than we do. We don't need to necessarily agree, but we need to sincerely understand them. That's empathy.

Our Negotiation Bedrock Concept 3, to Diagnose the Needs, is a critical initial step in the Negotiation Process. In this critical first step, Women are rock stars!!

WOMEN and the P.I.N. Iceberg

Women are more empathetic than men. This is no joke. It comes as second nature to women to show empathy and be concerned for others. Women have built-in features that make them think about others.

There are two proven reasons why women have more empathy than men. One is because of the body, and the other is because of the brain. More accurately, one is Neurological and the other Biochemical.

Neurological

We know the brains of females and males are structured differently. Studies have shown that men's brains are more connected within the same hemisphere while women's brains are more interconnected between different hemispheres, moving between the right and left sides of the brain. These neurological differences give light to behavioral and functional differences between the genders.

The neuroscientific Empathizing–Systemizing (E-S) theory perfectly explains the differences between these two orthogonal dimensions. The E-S theory explains that individual differences in the drive to empathize relative to the drive to systemize result from differences in the brain structure and connectivity of males and females.

Systemizing Quotient (SQ) is the drive to analyze systems in terms of the rules that govern them and the drive to construct systems – the appeal to understanding and predicting a system/situation or inventing a new one.

While Empathy Quotient (EQ) is the drive to identify others' emotions and thoughts and respond to them with an appropriate emotion – the appeal to understanding people.

The two hemispheres of a woman's brain talk to each other more than a man's brain, which allows for identifying emotions and thoughts, responding with appropriate emotion, and understanding the other person.

THE MALE AND FEMALE BRAIN

A new way of showing connectivity of the brain - called "connectome" maps - reveals significant difference between men and women

Typical male brain (top view) | **Typical female brain (top view)**

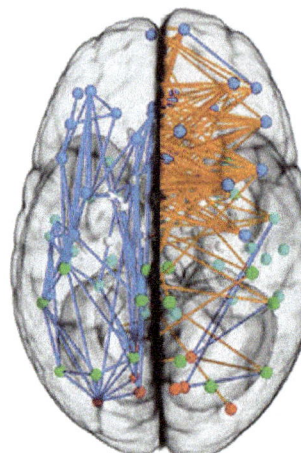

Most connections run between front and back parts of the same hemisphere. This could account for the better spatial skills and motor muscle control in men.

Many more neural connections go from side to side across the left and right hemispheres. Scientists say this could account for women's for better verbal skills and intuitive abilities.

The differences between the 'female brain' and the 'male brain,' according to Simon Baron-Cohen (University of Cambridge), emerged during the course of human evolution as each gender got exposed to different life challenges.

The male brain with systemizing tendencies (understanding and predicting a system/situation or inventing a new one) allowed for skills necessary for creating tools and weapons. But we can push the theory further in analyzing male emotion. More interestingly, the low empathy levels grew out of responding to long lone hunting trips and potentially committing acts of violence toward any competition – after all, it is much easier to kill said competition if you haven't connected on an emotional level.

Conversely, the female brain, characterized by empathizing tendencies (identifying emotions and thoughts and responding with appropriate emotion, understanding the other person to predict their behavior), offers much-needed skills for mothering infants who cannot communicate their needs directly.

Biochemical

Moving down from the brain to the body, we can look at the hormone connection that drives strong empathy in women.

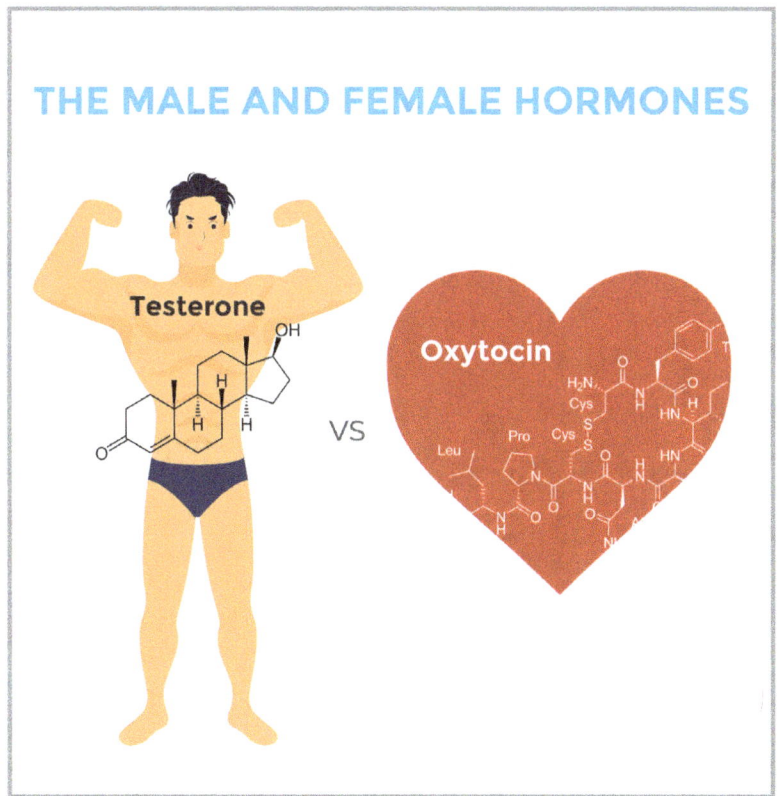

Testosterone, pinged as the male sex hormone, tends to make men feel more alpha, more competitive, and more likely to isolate themselves or initiate a confrontation.

Oxytocin, produced at higher levels in females, is dubbed the love hormone due to its role in social bonding. This hormone has various social and physiological functions in the brain and the body, promoting both maternal and social behavior, and enhancing relaxation.

When researchers analyzed data from hundreds of biological and behavioral studies, it was concluded that females were more likely to deal with stress by "tending and befriending" – that is, nurturing those around them and reaching out to others.

The brain and the body, the neurological makeup, and the biochemical, hormonal components make women more naturally equipped to engage, relate, and understand others – key skills for negotiating and influencing!

And critical for diagnosing the Needs – the Iceberg needs - of the Other Side.

Chapter 3 Summary

The belief that "The Other Person's problem is Solely Their Own" is the greatest Negotiation Myth of all time.

Skilled negotiators know the first step in moving towards the desired Outcome is diagnosing the NEEDS of the Other Party. We realize the existence of different levels of needs, and often, if not always, the ones under the waterline, the hidden, unspoken, subconscious needs are the ones really driving decisions and behavior.

To achieve our desired Outcome, we need to understand where the Other Party is coming from and what their true needs are. This would require the ability to relate and understand - it requires empathy and compassion. Caring about the Other Party makes us better negotiators. Women have the upper hand in this arena, and this is an ASSET!

W.I.N Negotiation Superpower 3: Keep Caring

In a negotiation, empathy is a superpower. The ability to care, see, understand, and empathize with the other side will not make us give up value at the table. Caring about the other side does not mean we will cave in or get sucked into giving in or being weak. Conversely, it means we will know how to move the Other Party forward. How to move that iceberg successfully.

Negotiation Tip!

To help Diagnose the Needs of the Counterparty, ask yourself, "What are they NOT saying?" This simple exercise will shift your thinking towards the right path.

Shhh! Don't Tell

It's 5:15am, and pitch-black is giving way to deep orange. You can barely see as tears stream down your face. Your fingers are starting to bleed, your thighs are on fire. You are on the brink of control. You accept the speed, hear the rhythm, and the pace makes sense.

The Outcome for one is the Outcome for the other. Mutual respect. You are looking after each other. You have found a higher ground of value and worth.

The back of a racehorse is an interesting place.

What strikes you about this sign?

The irony is that specifically what the sign tells people not to do is exactly what they did: throw stones at the sign. The statement on the sign provoked people to do exactly that.

Why? How?

From a psychological standpoint, what's happening here, and why do we, as negotiators, care? As it turns out, there is a reason our inner rebel can be sparked, or we feel a need to push back on authority.

Experts call this feeling or need to rebel Psychological Reactance. It's our brain's reaction when we feel a threat to our freedom or think our choices are being limited. When people feel that their choices are restricted or that others tell them what to do, they may feel a great need to rebel and do the opposite.

Psychological Reactance is a basic fear-based response to having no options or feeling a lack of freedom. It's the reason why *a* child sometimes does the opposite of what he is told. Why a person sometimes dislikes receiving a favor. Even health communication experts note that Psychological Reactance sometimes happens in response to health campaigns that tell people to quit smoking, or a very recent example, get a vaccine. "Don't tell me what to do, especially with my body!"

Essentially, when we tell someone what to do, there are four possible Outcomes:

- The first possible option is that they listen to argue - to disprove what is being said. They listen with the intent to poke holes in what they hear. Lawyers are trained to do this and do this well!

- The second possible option is that they don't listen at all - they tune out mentally. They start thinking about a grocery list, lunchtime snack, work project – anything but the subject being laid out before them.

- A third option could be that they don't listen at all, and this time, they physically walk/move away. This can be everything from physically moving away to muting the button and turning off the camera in the zoom meeting while they go for a coffee or bathroom break.

- And the last option, they may listen and agree.

Skilled negotiators consider the phenomenon of Psychological Reactance and work it to get their preferred Outcome. When aiming to influence another, we need to consider these response options and the likelihood of getting our Outcome and determine a strategic approach.

Regardless of how right we believe we are, how excited we are with our message, or how strong our case is, we will have a better Outcome if we can pull the answer out of the Other Party instead of pushing our point onto them. If we can bait them to come forward to our conclusion, we will be able to create and claim value. As skilled negotiators, we must consider organizing the communications so that our idea appears to come from them: Letting them, seemingly, voluntarily choose our preferred Outcome as their own.

An Italian diplomat was famous for saying it so succinctly: "Let them have our way."

To do this, we need to let them come up with the answers and tell us. We need to set this up with patience and discipline. Refrain from blurting out the answers but rather ask the right questions and say the right things so that they can TELL us what the answer is and what to do.

Negotiation Bedrock Concept 4

Skilled Negotiators understand Psychological Reactance. They Don't Tell, they Ask.

There are plenty of benefits to setting up communication this way, to asking rather than telling:

- We avoid Reactance – we avoid the pushback that happens when the Other Party feels a loss of freedom.

- We build in compliance - after all, this was "their" idea. The idea came from them.

- We enjoy concession trade - because it was "their" idea, we can ask for something valuable in return.

- Extra value for us - because it was "their" idea, we have no accountability or liability. We can claim value on the back-end if it doesn't totally go according to plan or delivers a less than perfect result.

- We establish rapport - because we are buying into their idea (which is our idea 😉), our agreement with their ideas would help build a rapport of big-time collaboration.

The benefits of executing communication this way and asking rather than telling are so numerous. What then is the problem? Why not ask questions?

One of the fears that comes from asking questions is losing control of the narrative. Suddenly, you find yourself discussing something you have no interest in, something that will not help you get your desired outcome.

One way to work the 'Don't Tell, Ask' strategy, in this case, is to give the Other Party options, all of which are acceptable to you. Also known as MESO (Multiple Equivalent Simultaneous Offers). Let the Other Party know the options (all acceptable to you), and then have them tell you the one they want. You can then confirm their option as their choice and build in compliance.

For example, a mother wanting to have the child wear their mittens to keep their fingers warm could ask the child:

Mother: *"Which mittens do you want to wear: the blue ones, the greens ones, the purple gloves, or the terrible black ones that you love so much?"*

I'd bet many kids would choose the "terrible black ones" – which would be fine – as all the options are acceptable to the mother.

A follow-up compliance measure would look like this: *"you chose the black mittens, so wear them!"*

Another big reason asking questions tends to get "the pushback" is because of the human ego. No one wants to appear stupid or like they don't know the answers. Less skilled negotiators often fall into this trap and argue their point, focusing on being right rather than the Outcome. This is where ego can cost a whole bunch!

WOMEN and Don't Tell, Ask.

Free from the Male Ego- Yahoo!

Taking the time to set the stage and build a questioning strategy that would lure the Other Party to your outcome is a lot to ask of oneself. This can be difficult, especially when the answer is clearly right in front of you and could be so easily and simply communicated. It requires discipline, focus, patience, and know-how.

Equally important, dare I say even more important, to the success of this strategy - of letting the Other Party take the lead, be right, and claim your idea as their own is the humility ability. For example, the ability to say: *"That's a great idea!"* while holding back the desire to correct and say, *"that's what I have been saying all along!"* The humility ability is the ability to allow the Other Party to be right, to have the answer. The ability to comfortably allow the Other Party to feel elevated without feeling that you have been put down.

We live in a culture that constantly promotes male supremacy. Long-held assumptions and stereotypes about masculinity and maleness have been unconsciously internalized by most men. Society shapes men's expectations of themselves, and to live up to these expectations, men continuously look for praise, attention, and recognition. The socially constructed and often frail male ego craves positive strokes. Many men are slaves to affirmation and acknowledgment of achievements or success.

Women, however, are free from the chains of the male ego. This allows for more freedom to let the Other Party take the lead and be seemingly right. As women, we are fundamentally more comfortable allowing the Other Party to come up with the answer and choose the direction (so long as it's ours). While this is a hard task for many men to achieve, it can be a walk in the park for many women.

Let's look at an example of dealing with Psychological Reactance and using our Bedrock Concept 4, 'Don't Tell, Ask,' to achieve our preferred outcome.

(Head's up! – this is an example to showcase the concept only!)

Scenario: DATE NIGHT

It is Thursday night, and it is date night at my house. My husband, Eric, and I usually connect as he drives home from work. I often call him while he is caught up in heavy traffic and a little annoyed as he just wants to get home.

On that Thursday night, I really wanted to go see the movie Bohemian Rhapsody. I didn't want to cook at home. I also didn't want to argue with my hubby. So, for the sake of this example, we'll define my desired Outcome as going to the Bohemian Rhapsody movie, going out for dinner and maintaining a good relationship. I knew that he would rather go see the A Star Is Born movie.

We can illustrate my desired Outcome by placing the three objectives (mentioned above) in the top section of the frame. It would look like this:

We can illustrate what I believe to be his desired Outcome by placing, what I believe to be his objective in the bottom left corner of the frame. It would look like this:

Now, imagine I found an article in the paper that rated the movies and claimed that Bohemian Rhapsody was up for an academy award. Very excited at the news and believing it to help my cause, I called my husband on the phone on his way home, and I said:

"We should go to Bohemian Rhapsody tonight, it has all these awards, and it is awesome."

By **telling** him this, I should expect one of four possible response outcomes:

1. He could agree. "Okay, if you say so, let's go." Even in this best-case scenario, I now owe him because it was my idea. All the liability is on my shoulders. If the movie is bad, it's my fault. I have no compliance built-in, and there is a good chance he may change his mind when he gets home, and we have a real conversation. His 'yes' may be what we can call a counterfeit yes.

2. He would not listen – mentally tune out. Not hear a word I said and change the subject.

3. He would not listen – physically push away. *"I can't talk now."*

4. He would listen and then argue – *"No, it is not awesome. A Star is Born is better,"* effectively building a "Blocker Wall" to my preferred Outcome.

We can illustrate the Blocker Wall like this:

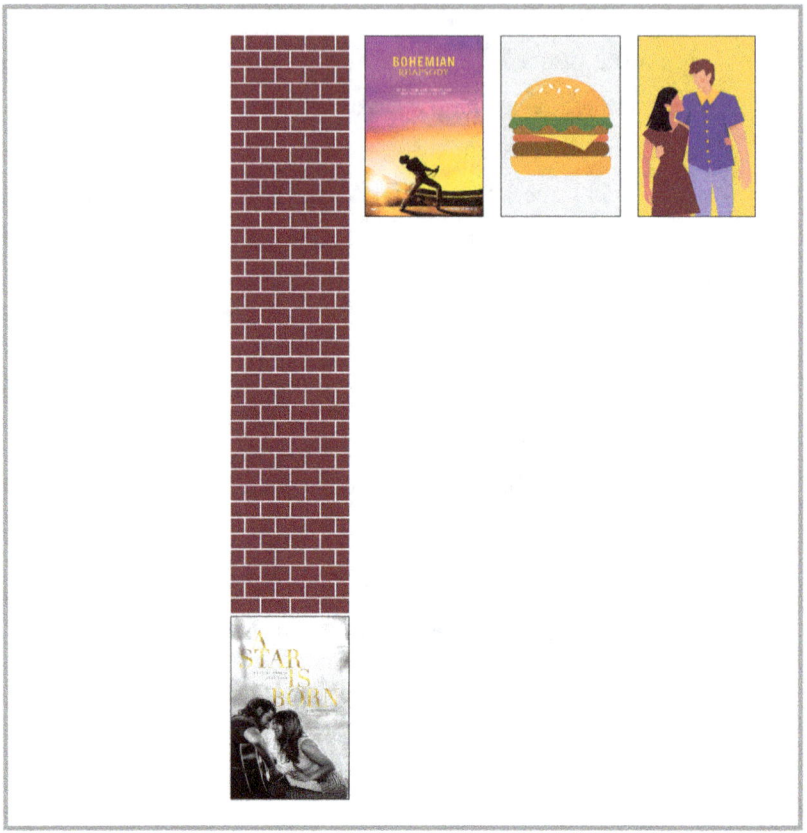

Less skilled negotiators would now attempt to break down that blocker wall, and they would get caught up in the "content quicksand." A typical scenario might play out like this:

> *Eric: "No, Bohemian Rhapsody is NOT awesome. A Star is Born is better."*

Me: "Well, actually, it's not. Bohemian Rhapsody has already won ABC, plus the lead actors are better, and the music is unbeatable."

*Eric: "Unbeatable? Lady Gaga is unbeat-
able. Plus, you can't get more relevant."*

And on and on it goes.

This conversation only makes the blocker wall bigger and thicker, therefore reducing the likelihood of achieving my desired Outcome: to push through the wall or jump over it.

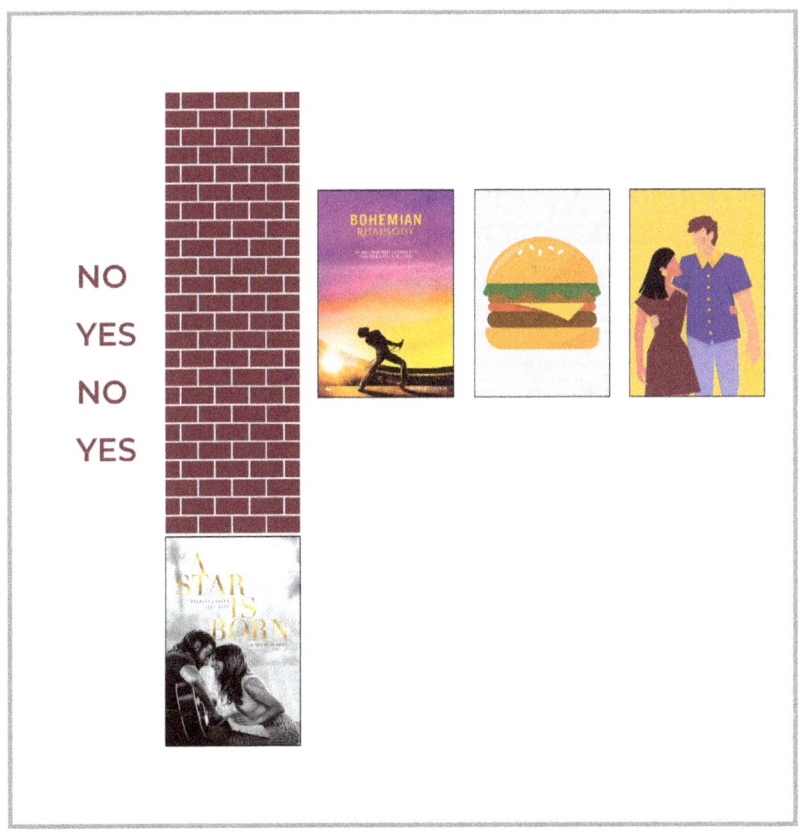

Alternatively, we could do the following:

Manage the **PROCESS** Strategy and avoid the sole obsession with the content (Negotiation Bedrock Concept 1). Execute our **Don't Tell, Ask,** strategy with Humility (Negotiation Bedrock Concept 4) after **Diagnosing his Needs** and empathizing with him (Negotiation Bedrock Concept 3), all the while trusting our **Intuition** (Negotiation Bedrock Concept 2) that tells us not to talk about how his workday was!

Now, the scenario could play out like this:

Instead of telling the Other Party (my hubby in this case) what we should do, I bide my time with discipline and strategy, bearing his needs in mind.

I wait until he is home, relaxed, and with a beer in hand. I place the New York Times review outlining Bohemian Rhapsody awards in front of him. I ASK him what the review says and allow him to TELL me about the movie review.

I then ASK him, "What do you feel like doing tonight?" Lo and behold, I just might get my Outcome right then and there.

See below:

As skilled negotiators, keeping Reactance in mind and employing our 'Don't Tell, Ask' strategy keeps us climbing that blocker wall. Because the idea (supposedly) came from him, we now can create and claim more value for ourselves.

Take a look –

We can 'give in' to his request to go to our movie and then ask for the aisle seat.

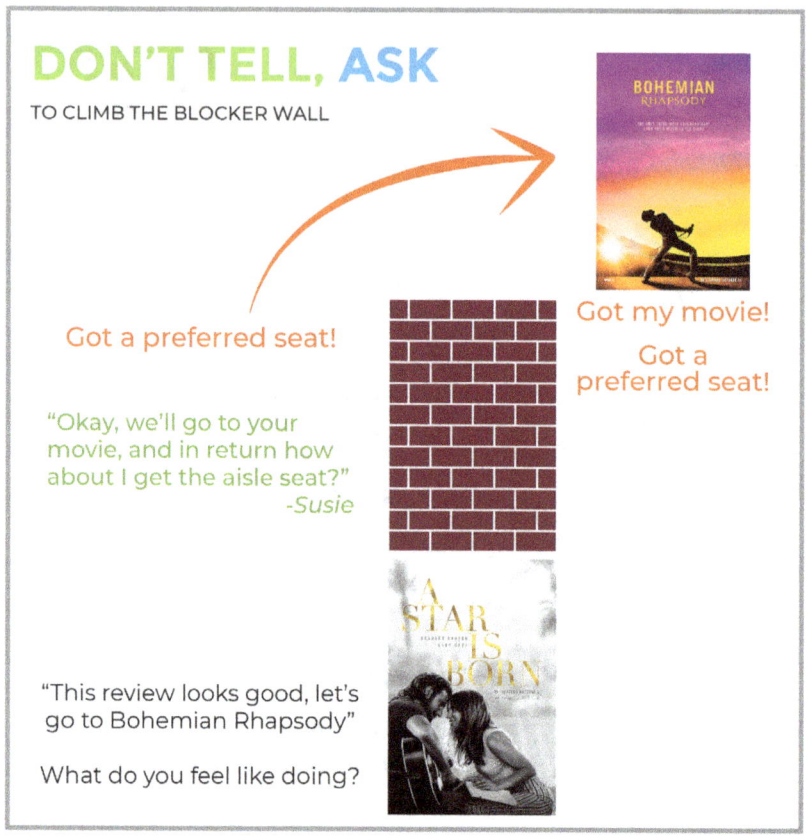

Let's keep climbing that wall, creating and claiming more value for ourselves and driving towards our preferred Outcome.

We can offer him a list of all the options that are acceptable to us. We ask him where he wants to go eat and let him choose. This way, the outcome we want, to go out for dinner, would be achieved regardless of what restaurant he chooses. We win in every case.

Now we have obtained our preferred movie, our preferred seat, and our dining out objective. We took our time, and with discipline, process control, and a question strategy, we guided the Other Party to our preferred Outcome. This built a climate of cooperation and agreement and enabled us to claim relationship equity. It also provides us with the opportunity to claim a future promised concession.

"I'm happy we are doing what you want tonight. Next week will be my turn."

We also strengthened our relationship and secured a concession for the following week. We can rest and relax knowing that it is not "on us" if the movie or the dinner is not up to snuff!

This is a crazy little scenario. Remember that the point is not about if this would ever happen. The point is that by understanding the phenomenon of Psychological Reactance and how it affects behavior, it may very well behoove us to take our time and think about how we can allow the Other Party to come up with the idea/solution. At the very least, part of the idea.

If we successfully get them to choose our preferred Outcome, we could build and claim more value for ourselves and build in compliance and accountability on their side. To do this, we must free ourselves from the need to be right. We must give up the need to fuel our own ego and get comfortable allowing the Other Party to be right. We must be humble and let the Other Party TELL us what to do.

Chapter 4 Summary

The very high-value concept of applying Psychological Reactance to the negotiation strategy and allowing/ setting it up so that the Other Party chooses our way requires an abandonment of ego and steadfast focus on the Outcome.

The male ego is a social construct resulting in the requirement/seeking of affirmation for achievement and success. Instead of fighting that ego, skilled negotiators employ the 'Don't Tell, Ask!' strategy.

A key asset in employing this strategy correctly is the Humility Ability. The ability to surrender from ego and allow the Other Party to give you the answer. Women have the advantage as they do not need to continuously have their egos stroked. In a negotiation situation, humility is a power play, which, when recognized in yourself, is a superpower.

W.I.N Negotiation Superpower 4: Give in! 😌 And let them have "your" way.

Negotiation Tip!

When dealing with certain types of defiant personalities, a useful tactic to drive the Counterparty to accept your position is to suggest an 'alternative' (Yikes!) or actually promote the alternative (double Yikes!)

Negotiation Tip!

It is important to keep a check on our own Reactance if you find yourself pushing back on something someone is telling you. Listen, truly listen to what they are saying to determine if your pushback is coming from a place of Reactance.

Negotiation Tip!

When asking the questions, remember to listen. Truly listen. We may find/discover a novel idea, an elegant new solution that answers each other's needs.

Negotiation Tip!

Sometimes, the best approach is to use straight shooter communication. This remains an option. It may even be the best option based on the situation and your preferred Outcome. Remember your approach is a strategic decision.

Go Ahead, Underestimate Me

Grace like no other.

*Silky-smooth coat, the mane that blows in the
wind and rocks up and down in stride*

*Black hooves tipped at the end of long legs, as
like polished black tap-dancing shoes*

The nicker, the whinny - symbolic of the ultimate feminine cry.

The rear, the gallop, the buck.

The most magnificent beauty — this is the horse.

noooooo......

The glory of her nostrils is terrible.

*She tears through the valley and rejoices in her power
and shoves her muscle.*

She swallows the ground with fierceness and rage.

She is swifter than leopards,

fiercer than the evening wolves.

This is the horse.

Negotiation Bedrock Concept 5

It takes only 7 seconds to form an opinion, and 93% of these opinions are based on nonverbals. Women can use this to their advantage!

The Other Party will form an impression of you within the first 7 seconds of the first interaction, and only 7% of what you say is included in that calculation. The other 93% will be based on the physical.

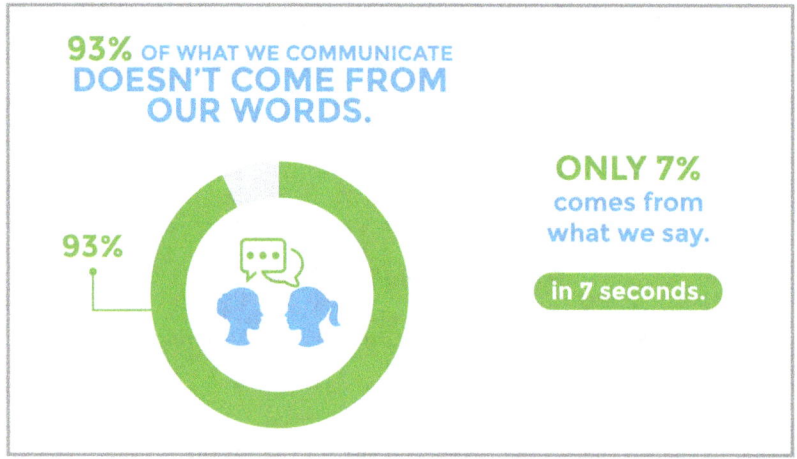

People are quick to jump to conclusions and make assumptions. Partly because people can be mentally lazy and are often in a hurry. We have no time to waste to consider or challenge our comfortable conceptions. It is easier to think we know. Yet, making assumptions in negotiation can cause defeat. It's no wonder that many of our mistakes are carefully planned out!

Skilled negotiators are aware of this potential pitfall and ensure to test and check assumptions. Higher skilled negotiators seek to use the potential pitfall to their benefit. They are aware of the potential advantages of not correcting the Other Party's false perceptions. If played well, assumption, correction & exploitation can be a game-changer in a negotiation. That is why the Negotiation Preparation Methodology devotes an entire step to the strategic management of assumptions.

The Negotiation Preparation Methodology offers us a step-by-step guide to a successful negotiated Outcome.

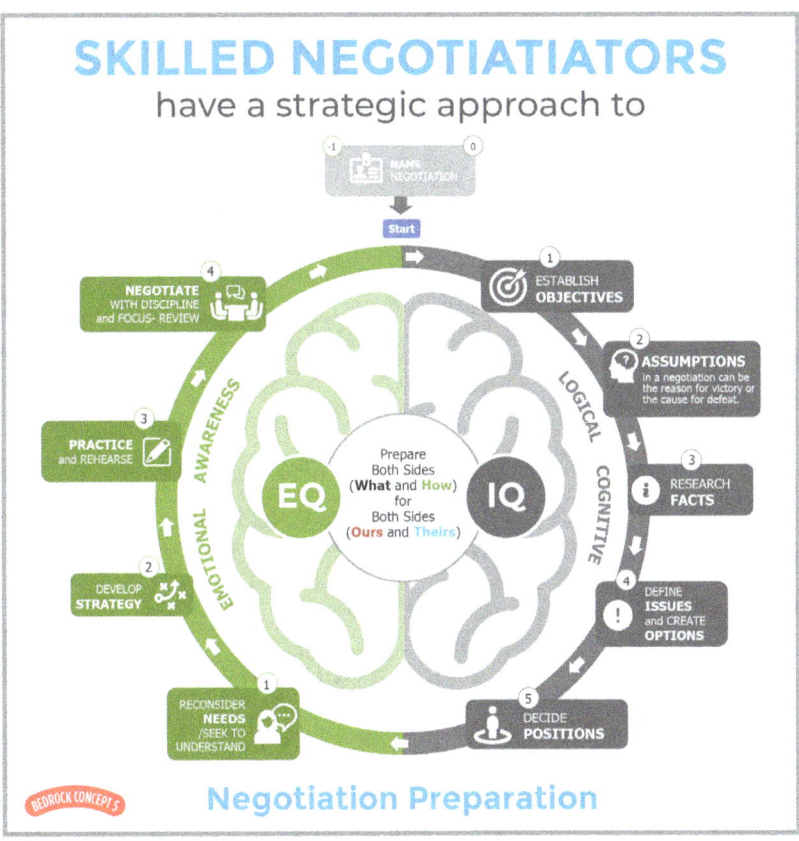

The methodology cleverly depicts negotiation as a wheel. This is because a negotiation is very seldom a one-off event but rather consists of a number of smaller negotiations making it serial in nature, and ongoing. Some contemporary schools of thought submit it would be better represented as a sphere to include and consider the side chats, concurrent events, and other negotiations going on at the same time that can affect your Outcome.

The first half of the negotiation wheel focuses on the logical and cognitive part - the Substance component, while the other half focuses on the emotional and people part- the Process.

The second step on the Substance side of the methodology is devoted to Assumptions: correction and exploitation. One helpful activity is to list all the assumptions we are making- create an exhaustive list. Next, rank each of the assumptions according to their potential impact on the Outcome of the negotiation; high, medium low risk. Then, determine the best way (who, when, where, how) to test them. Afterwards list all the assumptions the Other Party may have made and determine what to do with their assumptions: test them, correct them, ignore them or use them?

The Identify & Test Assumption exercise helps us answer key questions such as what assumptions are we making as individuals and as a team? Are they high or low-risk assumptions? How can we avoid surprises? What is the best way to test each assumption?

This exercise also helps us build a picture of what the Other Party is thinking, feeling, and believing. What assumptions is the Other Party making about:

- Facts, rules, constraints, procedures, budgets?
- Rationality, equity, ethics, credibility, trust?
- Power, authorities, timeframes?

- Stereotypes, cultural variances, prejudices?

- Our BATNAs (Our Best Alternatives to Negotiated Agreement)?

- Assumptions about relationships, linkages, and people.

About people? About us??

Is the Other Party making assumptions we can use to our advantage??

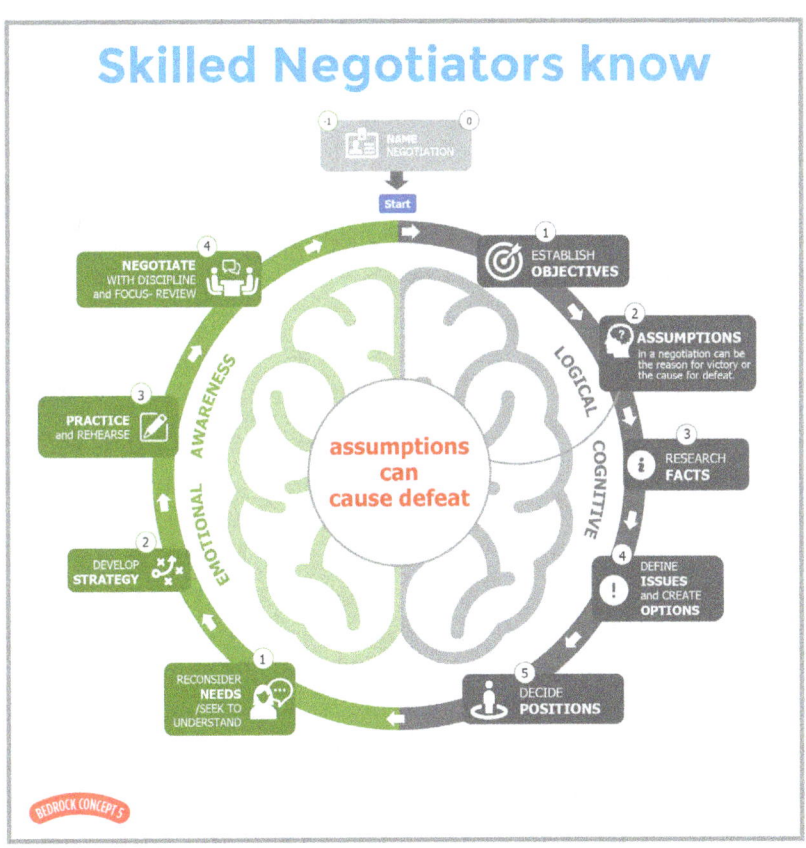

WOMEN and Assumptions

One of the most dangerous assumptions in a negotiation is assuming the Other Party is less than they are. Underestimating the Other Party can prompt one to make sloppy mistakes, say too much, lose focus of the Outcome, fail to plan, fail to find options, and much more. Because when one believes there is no contest, rarely will one compete.

When we look at male-female physical differences, we see that women are mostly lighter and smaller-framed, their voices are softer, their skin is thinner, their jaw is narrower, they are less hairy, less scary!

Women are more exposed. We can't hide our faces behind a beard or bushy eyebrows. Our thinner skin allows the Other Party to see our face changes (turning red or white) due to an emotion of fright, surprise, or embarrassment.

Also, the socially accepted dressing makes women even more vulnerable – wrists are exposed, necks, angles, and jugulars – are all exposed.

So, what does this mean? What do we do? As negotiators, what action should we take?

One option is to work on increasing our macho presence, add male gravitas, and become bigger. We could work on ways to take more space, more oxygen. We could practice the power pose. This would increase our testosterone levels and lower cortisol levels, both of which come from standing like a scarecrow for two minutes! However, adopting the "Fake it 'till You Make It" move will only work in the short term for short periods of time, at best.

Pretending to be something or someone you are not will eventually and undoubtedly take its toll. It may even start to poke at your own self-respect and get recklessly close to disrupting your dignity.

Another option, the W.I.N option, is to not worry about changing things we have no control over, things we could never compete with, but rather embrace our authentic selves and find empowerment there. So instead of "Fake it 'till You Make It," don't fake it at all! Reverse it and use what we have to our advantage; we potentially have the benefit of being assumed weaker, vulnerable, softer, even breakable.

Look at it through the W.I.N lens – Let's not correct the Other Party's assumption.

Instead of trying to be bigger at the table, take up more room, or have more gravitas and presence- let's not. Let's allow them to assume, let them underestimate us. Let's allow our physical to bait the Other Party into underestimating us.

Be unapologetically you. If that moves the Other Party to pay half attention and make sloppy mistakes at the table, fail to do the needed research, fail to plan for alternatives, or even fail to invite the correct team members, so be it. If you are underestimated because of your femininity, then so be it. Your energy capital is better spent focusing on the negotiation at hand versus correcting their assumptions.

Why fix the Other Party's mistake with the **"Don't you dare underestimate me!"** sentiment. Instead, sit back, embrace every girly thing about you, and allow assumptions to lead to underestimating just how strong you can be. **"Go ahead, underestimate me. That will be fun!"**

Underestimate me.
That'll be fun.

Never underestimate the power in being underestimated.
Susie Maloney, Negotiation Architect, Blu Bonsai

It may all end up getting corrected, or it may not. But even if it does, we should have a good head start down the strategic path!

Chapter 5 summary

It takes only 7 seconds to form an opinion, and 93% of these opinions come from nonverbals. Women, for the most part, appear physically softer than men. Our bodies signal that we would rather not fight. This can lead the Other Party into making big (and wrong) assumptions about us.

One option is to attempt to change the Other Party's perception of us. We could use tactics to build our gravitas and presence. However, there could be a better way to navigate to a successful Outcome, and that is to allocate all our focus and energy on the negotiation and leave the Other Party to maintain false assumptions.

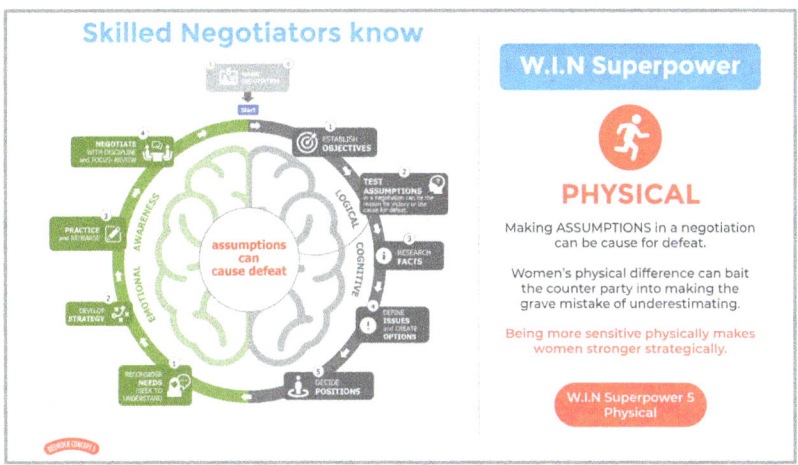

W.I.N Negotiation Superpower 5: Use the Physical

Embrace every girly thing about you and allow assumptions to lead the Other Party to underestimating just how strong you can be. It all may end up getting corrected, or it may not. But even if it does, you should have a good head start down the strategic path.

A few bonus benefits to our physical:

The fact that women are smaller, less seen, and more under the radar allows women to pick up all sorts of insights that may be missed by the one who is used to being center stage. In a negotiation, unseen and in the corner can be the greatest seat of all.

Being softer looking and giving off an aura of "nice" makes us more approachable. This can allow the Other Party to come to us with their guards down and share important information and insights.

Women are physically more sensitive- women have thinner skin and greater nerve density. Women can sense mood shifts in a room and play it strategically to their advantage. Women can easily pick up changes in body temperatures or the moisture in the room, all signs of an emotional mood shift.

Authenticity gives you power in and of itself. Realizing that you are all you need gives confidence from within and allows you to allocate resources such as energy, time, and mindshare on the tasks at hand.

Being more sensitive physically makes women stronger strategically.

CHAPTER SIX

The Female Five

Masters of sensory awareness and processing: An average horse weighs about 1,200 pounds. They are quick and strong. They have hooves and teeth. Yet, with the humility of a servant, they allow you to move their thousand pounds of muscle as you wish.

They don't question how they feel about a situation because they are designed to listen and trust their instincts. They are all about intuition and empathy. Their lives depend on it.

They can read your energy even before you come close to them. They understand your feelings, which gives them the confidence to allow you to ride them to achieve your Outcome.

The Female Five

It's nothing new.

IT IS SAID that Negotiation is as old as the hills. Research predates bargaining behavior to the time Homo sapiens were developed as species. We saw proofs of communication of trading and exchanging chiseled on cave walls. Interestingly, the actual study of Negotiation is not new either. We've been studying the behavior, trying to make sense of it all for thousands of years. The amount of research and theory that has gone into explaining the negotiation behavior is overwhelming, and it is impossible to know it all. The good news is you don't need to know it all and what you need to know, you already know! You already have it!

W.I.N just gives you a way to find it in yourself!

Within the first half-hour of working with a new client or team, I share that my objective is to make them better negotiators and influencers at the end of our time together. I always feel it is silly to say this because it is obvious that that should be my objective. The nuance is that I'm not focused on ensuring that they understand the negotiation theory. I'm not even concerned if they fully and completely understand the findings (models, frameworks, and concepts) that we uncover and unpack together. For them to be better negotiators, the work we do together needs to be transferable, memorable, and dependable. **Transferable:** readily available to them throughout their work and life. **Memorable:** it sticks with them beyond our time together and grows more useful over time. **Dependable:** it must come to them at times when they need it the most. This can be when they are stressed, tired, or overwhelmed. Perhaps how one feels amid a heated negotiation?

When you are in the heat of an interaction, you do not have time to press pause and hit the books. The complex theory and negotiation findings need to be rolled up in memorable models that are easy to remember and easy to find in your mind – right in your moment of need!

Grounded in research and theory, born from behavioral science and psychology, W.I.N examines 5 key bedrock negotiation concepts, then hones and refines them through a highly practical experience-based approach. W.I.N looks at what characteristics skilled negotiators exhibit with respect to these concepts and the distinct advantages women have (or can have!) to win in the negotiation arena. The tools and techniques, models, and frameworks are built to be transferable, memorable, and dependable.

W.I.N examines 5 key bedrock negotiation concepts, what characteristics skilled negotiators exhibit with respect to these concepts, and the indisputable uniqueness women have to win in the negotiation arena.

Dual Competencies & Multitasking

Capitalize on your Mental and Sensory **Multitasking** skills to simultaneously use your IQ and EQ. This will help you master the dual competencies (the WHAT and the HOW) of negotiation.

Perception Shaping & Intuition

Appreciate **Intuition** as an asset. It is your personal GPS available 24/7. Listen to it and trust it during orchestrated and unorchestrated events at and away from the table.

Needs Diagnosis & Empathy

Embrace **Empathy** strategically to dig down and uncover, diagnose, and truly understand the needs of the other side. Until we do, we may stay stuck.

Psychological Reactance & Humility

Steer the Other Party's ego and allow them the chance to TELL you. Allow them the chance to be the one to be "right." Lift them up with your **Humility** Ability.

Assumptions & the Physical

Physical; you are all you need. If the Other Party doesn't see you, focus on the Outcome you want, and think strategy before correcting assumptions.

Negotiating Superpowers Wrap up – *Authenticity*
It's about you.

The "Big N" is what we call the formal, at-the-table time zone. During this interaction time zone, we pass through four distinct phases known as the Introductory, Discovery, Integration, and Settlement phases. Skilled negotiators clearly understand that specific objectives are to be reached during each of these phases, and each phase must be managed and paced accordingly. One of the key objectives for the Introductory phase is to get to know each other on a more personal level. Find some early personal common ground: could be the weather, sports team, college, clothes, etc. This phase gives the negotiator a chance to set a tone, break/erect barriers, find out information, plant information, and more. We suggest not to rush this phase. Small talk can be extremely useful during this phase, and skilled negotiators know this.

However, not everyone is comfortable with this phase. While working with an accomplished senior leader in Washington D.C in preparation for their "Big N," they confided in me that they were quite shy as a person and not at all comfortable with personal small talk. They were easily off balanced when it came to personal chatting with people they didn't know well. So, for them, the Introductory phase was stressful, almost a liability. In this case, we decided the best course of action to get the Outcome we wanted was to allow the peripheral team to take on the Introductory phase and use the time variable to our advantage by having the senior leader join the negotiation at a later stage. In this case, the "Big N" model did not work for them.

Some Negotiation concepts, frameworks, tools, and techniques will be helpful to you. Others may not. The key is to take what works for you, for the situation and use it, alter, or leave the rest. It's about using what works for YOU to be a better negotiator. Just like the stars, the trees, and the snowflakes, you are unique. There is no two You. What makes you a good negotiator is not the same as what makes another a good negotiator. No one and no model or concept can tell you how to be You. The models and concepts are only there for you to use the ones that work for you and the situation.

At the end of the day, the real superpower is Authenticity.

Authenticity breeds self-confidence and guards against intimidation. Moreover, being your authentic self allows you to channel your energy in the right direction. It gives you the license to tap into your strengths and not bother about going against your gut because a book (or your boss) says so.

Be yourself and tap into your unique talents. Being your authentic self will make you happy, and this happiness creates a special energy that attracts others to you with positive reactions. Others will follow you naturally towards your ideas and preferred Outcomes.

That's a negotiation superpower!

You've got this!

But you know that already. W.I.N just gives you a way to think about it.

Key Bedrock Negotiation Concepts & The Female Five

About the Author

Susie Maloney is an International Professional Negotiator, Negotiation Strategist and Architect born in Ottawa, Canada. She moved with her family to Cameroon as a young child and then returned to Canada for her formative years. She attended the University of Ottawa and received her first degree in ECONOMICS. She went on to ride for the Canadian team – she was part of the Canadian Olympic Equestrian Team and served as a reserve rider for Barcelona in 1992.

She is an adored keynote speaker, a frequent lecturer and an Adjunct Professor at the Business School level, as well as an esteemed Judge for the Halloum Negotiation Competition at UC Berkeley, California. She is highly trained in the areas of Negotiation and Influencing ***strategy and process*** and currently leads the Negotiating Strategies training for the Complex Project & Procurement Executive Leadership program at the University of Ottawa, Canada, her alma mater.

Often described by clients as their best-kept secret, Susie works both on the front lines and behind the scenes with governments and large multinationals and conglomerates on high-stake interactions to resolve often difficult, multi-lateral issues involving diverse stakeholders with disparate needs.

The tools, techniques, models, and frameworks she uses are grounded in research and theory born from behavioral science and psychology, then honed and refined through a highly practical experience-based approach. Susie doesn't teach nice theories – she discovers fundamental concepts through practical application and the analysis of what works.

Susie lives with her husband and two children in San Francisco, California, and Vancouver, BC, and is committed to empowering women and helping them succeed at the negotiation table. She is a provoker of original thought and a stubborn challenger of the status quo. Her ability to see the indisputable uniqueness women bring to the influencing process and how they are strengths – or can be - in the negotiation milieu is a great provoking presentation.

www.ingramcontent.com/pod-product-compliance
Lightning Source LLC
Chambersburg PA
CBHW062340290526
45794CB00005B/2064